Louis Jolliet

Jacques Marquette

THE WORLD'S GREAT EXPLORERS

Jacques Marquette and Louis Jolliet

By Zachary Kent

Marquette at St. Ignace de Michilimackinac, 1673

Project Editor: Mark Friedman

Designer: Lindaanne Donohoe

Photo Editor: Jan Izzo

Cover Art: Steven Gaston Dobson

Engraver: Liberty Photoengraving

**Library of Congress
Cataloging-in-Publication Data**

Kent, Zachary
   Jacques Marquette and Louis Jolliet/Zachary Kent.
      p.   cm. — (The World's great explorers)
   Includes bibliographical references (p.   ) and index.
   Summary: An account of the expedition led by two
Frenchmen to explore the Mississippi River in the
late seventeenth century.
   ISBN 0-516-03072-8
   1. Marquette, Jacques, 1637-1675—Juvenile
literature. 2. Jolliet, Louis, 1645-1700—Junvenile
lieterature. 3. Canada—History—To 1763 (New
France)—Juvenile literature. 4. Mississippi River
Valley—History—To 1803—Juvenile literature.
5. Explorers—America—Biography. 6. Explorers—
France—Biography. [1. Marquette, Jacques, 1637-
1675. 2. Jolliet, Louis, 1645-1700. 3. Explorers. 4.
Mississippi River—Discovery and exploration.]
   I. Title. II. Series.

F1030.2.K44   1994   92-36888
977—dc20   CIP
[B]   AC

Marquette and Jolliet on the Mississippi

Table of Contents

Chapter 1
The Big River

Native American men, women, and children ran to the riverbank. They waved their arms and shouted greetings to seven Frenchmen in two birchbark canoes. The canoes glided across the water until their bows finally touched the shore.

The Menominee gazed at the packed canoes and hoped they carried trading goods such as muskets, hatchets, and knives. Six of the Frenchmen wore buckskins or the rough woolen clothes and knit caps of traders. Their leader was sturdy, twenty-seven-year-old Louis Jolliet, a skilled mapmaker and explorer. The seventh traveler wore the long, black robe of a Jesuit priest. Tall and lean, thirty-five-year-old Father Jacques Marquette smiled at the Indians as he stepped among them.

Less than two weeks earlier, on May 17, 1673, these explorers had set out from the mission of St. Ignace at Michilimackinac on an important expedition. They were in search of the Mississippi River, which no Frenchman had ever seen.

The St. Lawrence River in Quebec

The geography of North America remained a mystery to Europeans in the 1600s. England, Spain, and France all laid claims to vast unexplored sections of territory. Along the St. Lawrence River in Canada, French pioneers had chopped down trees and cleared land for farms and trading posts. Each year French traders pushed farther west in search of valuable furs. French missionaries ventured into the wilderness in an attempt to introduce the Roman Catholic religion to the Native Americans.

The Indians had told French explorers stories of a river called the Mississippi, "The Big River," and in 1672, the French colonial government appointed Louis

Jolliet to find and explore the fabled river. With Father Marquette and five trading partners, Jolliet journeyed to the nation of the Menominee.

The Menominee chiefs stared with surprise when they learned the purpose of the Frenchmen's visit. The chiefs recommended that the explorers turn back rather than attempt to find the Big River. They feared the river as a mysterious place that was home to monsters and demons. They also warned the Frenchmen of Indians living along the river who were fierce warriors and would "never show mercy to strangers, but [would] break their heads without any cause . . ."

The raging Mississippi

The Fox River

The Frenchmen listened to these warnings, but were determined to go ahead in spite of any dangers. After handing out a few small gifts and collecting food supplies, they climbed into their canoes once more.

The explorers paddled south on Green Bay, and then on to the Fox River. They encountered the friendly Maskouten Indians, and with the help of two Native American guides, Marquette, Jolliet, and their companions forged further on the Fox River, eventually connecting with the Wisconsin River.

On June 17, 1673, the Frenchmen stared with awe as the Wisconsin River approached another larger river. This new river stretched a mile wide and flowed due south. This was surely the Big Water about which

The travelers enter the Mississippi.

the Indians spoke with such fear and respect. The voyagers allowed the gentle current to pull their canoes forward. "We safely entered the Mississippi," Father Marquette later wrote, ". . . with a Joy that I cannot Express."

The seven explorers became the first Frenchmen to reach the mighty Mississippi River. It was their duty now to follow its course southward and explore where it led. Many dangers and adventures awaited them. The trader Louis Jolliet was filled with brave curiosity, and the dedicated priest Jacques Marquette yearned to bring his religion to Indian nations. Together these two men welcomed the thrilling challenge of the Mississippi.

Chapter 2
The Education of a Jesuit

Jacques Marquette was born on June 1, 1637, in the city of Laon in northern France. Rose de la Salle Marquette gently cradled her baby in her arms, while Nicolas Marquette, a respected lawyer and landowner, smiled proudly at his son. The Marquettes already had two daughters, Marie and Francoise. After Jacques, three more boys would be born: Louis, Jean-Bertrand, and Charles. These six laughing children filled the Marquette house with joy.

When he reached the age of five, Jacques prepared for his first schooling. His mother dressed the sturdy youngster in skirts, according to the fashion of the 1600s. Each morning the boy carried his slate and pencil to the nearby church of St. Martin-au-Parvis. Jacques's uncle, Michel Marquette, served as a priest and teacher there. Seated at wooden desks, Jacques and other boys learned reading, writing, and arithmetic. On Sundays and holidays Jacques faithfully attended Roman Catholic Mass with his family. Thoughts of religion often filled his mind. In church and at home he learned about Roman Catholic missionaries. To spread their faith, these rugged priests traveled to the farthest reaches of the world and lived among the natives. To Jacques, the life of a missionary seemed one of bravery, glory, and excitement.

In 1646, the Marquettes enrolled nine-year-old Jacques in the fine Jesuit college at Reims. The Jesuit priests who ran the college were members of the Society of Jesus, a Roman Catholic order founded by Saint Ignatius Loyola in 1540. Jacques quickly made new friends and learned the school's daily routine. After morning prayers, he washed his face and dressed in his school uniform, a black robe tied around the waist with a red sash. He reviewed his schoolwork in his room until breakfast time. After sipping wine and eating bread, he hurried to his morning classes, which began at 8:00 and lasted until 10:30. Then all of the students respectfully filed into church for Mass. Cooks served the midday meal at 11:45. Jacques gulped hot soup and munched on beef, mutton, vegetables, bread, and maybe some pudding or pie for dessert.

Perhaps the happiest time of the day was the recreation period that followed. In the college courtyards the younger boys played blindman's bluff, checkers, tennis, and other games. Inside, students learned dancing, swordsmanship, and drawing. At 2:00 the boys returned to their formal studies, which lasted until the 6:00 supper bell. After a hearty meal, students relaxed and reviewed their books until 8:45. Night prayers marked the end of each day, and by 9:00 Jacques and his classmates climbed into their beds.

During his teenage years at the Jesuit college Jacques grew into a scholar. He learned such subjects as history, mathematics, geography, Latin, and classical Greek. When they finished their education, many of Jacques's classmates returned home to their family estates to live the lives of gentlemen. Other graduates became doctors, lawyers, and professors.

A Jesuit priest

Jacques, however, desired the life of a missionary. He wanted to join the Society of Jesus and serve in a foreign land. Over time, the Jesuits observed the young man, saw that he was sincere, and accepted his application to study for the Jesuit priesthood. For the apprentice program, called the novitiate, Jacques attended the Jesuit school in the French city of Nancy.

In October 1654, seventeen-year-old Jacques Marquette traveled by stagecoach to Nancy. Sixteen students arrived at the Jesuit novitiate school that fall. Many tasks lay before these young men before they could become Jesuit priests. For one month that autumn Jacques remained deep in prayer, making a special study of the life of Jesus Christ. He spent another month nursing the sick at a local hospital. Another young Jesuit wrote of this work: "We made the beds, swept the floors . . . cleaned up the wards . . . day and night, attended on the sick. . . ." This difficult service taught Jacques tenderness and charity.

Cathedral of Laon

Other Jesuit school duties made Jacques more humble. He assisted in the kitchen, stirring soup and baking bread. He cleaned the tables after meals and emptied sacks of garbage. On laundry days he sank his arms in soapy tubs filled with clothes and sheets. Jacques was the pampered son of a wealthy lawyer, so he had never performed such dirty chores. In order to become a priest and missionary, however, he gladly did this work.

During his second year as a Jesuit novice, Jacques fulfilled another test. He set out on a long pilgrimage with another student. The two young men hiked the dusty roads leading 100 miles (161 kilometers) to the German town of Trier. Neither of them carried so much as a single coin. Along the way they begged for food and lodging at farmhouses and village taverns. Some people greeted them with warmth and generosity. Others shouted angrily and turned the two beggars away from their doors.

Lean and suntanned, Jacques returned to Nancy. He had survived for a month by relying on his own faith and others' good will. The Jesuit priests at Nancy graded Jacques Marquette as an able, intelligent, and earnest young man. More work lay ahead, however, before nineteen-year-old Jacques could claim the title of Jesuit priest.

Outside the windows of the Jesuit college at Auxerre, the leaves were turning bright autumn colors on October 18, 1656. At the morning bell a group of eleven-year-old students filed into a classroom and met their new teacher—Master Marquette. Jacques quizzed his students in geography, drilled them in Latin and Greek, and corrected essay papers.

After a year of teaching at Auxerre, Marquette

returned to school himself. Starting in October 1657, he studied advanced courses in philosophy, physics, and mathematics at the Jesuit university at Pont-a-Mousson. After two years at Pont-a-Mousson, he returned to his old college at Reims to serve another two years as a teacher. From October 1661 to September 1665, he patiently taught school at Charleville, Langres, and again at Pont-a-Mousson.

By then Marquette had grown into a tall, serious twenty-seven-year-old man. As he lay in bed at night he sometimes wondered if he would ever become a missionary. He dreamed of sailing to China or some other foreign land to spread the Christian faith. He finally wrote to John Paul Oliva, the leader of the Jesuits, and begged for a chance.

In January 1666, joyous news reached Marquette. His Jesuit superior at Pont-a-Mousson showed him a letter from Father Oliva. "The Canadian mission is in desperate need of workers," Oliva wrote, ". . . Among others there is Master Marquette who can be sent at the first opportunity." On March 7, 1666, Marquette knelt in the cathedral at Toul and was ordained a Jesuit priest in a solemn ceremony. He then hurriedly packed his trunk. He visited Laon where, with smiles and tears, he kissed his parents good-bye.

Marquette traveled by stagecoach to La Rochelle. Dozens of ships crowded the harbor of that busy French seaport. In his black robes, the young priest excitedly walked along the wharves until he found the fleet bound for Canada. In August 1666, Father Jacques Marquette stood at the rail of one of seven ships that hoisted anchor and sailed west. Marquette gazed in wonder at the broad Atlantic Ocean—a new world awaited him on the other side.

Chapter 3
The Gentle Missionary

"Father Jacques Marquette arrived, in good health, on the seventh ship," penned Canadian priest Father Francois Le Mercier in his journal on September 20, 1666. The French fleet had plunged across the rolling ocean waves and had steered a careful course up the rocky St. Lawrence River. At last, after a six-week journey, the ships anchored in the harbor of Quebec. Two Jesuit priests rowed out and helped Marquette transfer his luggage to shore. Marquette followed along as they led him through the streets.

The young priest stared keenly in all directions. Shops and warehouses lined crooked lanes in Quebec's lower town beside the riverbank. Tailors, coopers, tinsmiths, and bakers all worked busily. Fur trappers wearing woolen stocking caps carried beaver pelts slung over their shoulders or sat outside tavern doorways drinking wine and smoking pipes. Marquette noticed Indians everywhere wearing beaded buckskin, sewn leggings, and colorful blankets. Quebec's population was less than 600, but the city seemed a very busy place.

France had first staked its claim to Canada in 1535 after explorer Jacques Cartier sailed up the St. Lawrence River. In 1608, Samuel de Champlain established a fort at Quebec. The town that grew around it became the capital of New France, France's Canadian colony.

The two Jesuits led Marquette up a steep road to the summit of a rocky plateau. Here stood Quebec's upper town of sturdy houses and handsome granite buildings. Marquette saw stonemasons building a new Roman Catholic church. His companions likely pointed out the Hotel Dieu that served as a hospital and the high walls of the governor's house called the Chateau St. Louis.

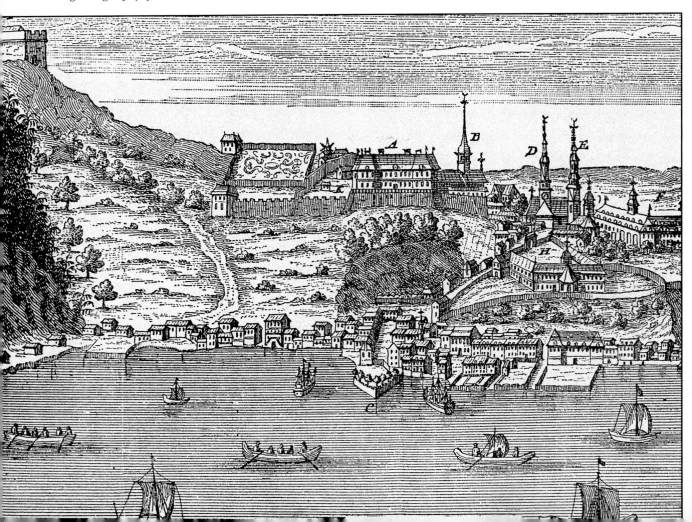

The growing city of Quebec

The two priests brought Marquette to Quebec's Jesuit college. Jesuit superior Father Francois Le Mercier and other priests warmly welcomed the new missionary. At supper these men described life in the colony. From Quebec, Three Rivers, Montreal, and other river settlements, French trappers and traders paddled away each spring in search of beaver. Furs of beaver were valued highly by European hatmakers. In the footsteps of the trappers followed the missionaries. The French missionaries believed Roman Catholicism was the only true faith. They felt that if they could convert the Native Americans from their own religions to Catholicism, they could save the Indians' souls. The priests had preached successfully among the Algonquian and Huron Indians who lived north and west of the St. Lawrence River. The Jesuits also hoped to open missions deeper in the western frontier. Before taking part in that work, however, Father Marquette needed to learn at least one of the Indian languages. On October 10, Father Le Mercier recorded in his journal, "Father Jacques Marquette goes up to Trois-Rivieres [Three Rivers] to be a pupil of Father Druilletes. . . ."

Chilly autumn breezes filled the sails of the little boat that carried Marquette 80 miles (129 km) up the St. Lawrence River. The boat docked at the frontier town of Three Rivers. Marquette trudged through the muddy streets and arrived at the Jesuit mission, where Father Gabriel Druillettes happily greeted him. The priest was busy and could use the help of a young apprentice.

A few hundred Algonquian Indians lived in cabins near the Jesuit mission. These Indians had chosen to adopt the ways of the French. Each morning at dawn Father Marquette called them to the mission chapel.

Father Marquette

He listened carefully as they recited their prayers in their native language. Later in the day the children chanted their lessons aloud at the mission school. They giggled at Father Marquette's mistakes as he learned their Algonquian words.

Father Le Mercier soon realized that Marquette was ready for greater responsibilities. ". . . Father Jacques Marquette," he wrote, "has a good knowledge of Algonquian . . . is of sound health and strong body. . . and because of his wonderfully gentle ways, [is] most acceptable to the natives."

In the spring of 1668, Marquette finally received new orders. He was to journey west to the Great Lakes along with Brother Louis Böeme and two other young church workers. Ottawa Indians from that region had arrived at Three Rivers to trade furs. When they left for home at summer's end, they gladly allowed the four Frenchmen to travel with them.

The Ottawa Indians steered their canoes up the St. Lawrence River, past the island town of Montreal, and up the Ottawa River. The travelers were often forced to portage—carry the canoes and gear overland for short distances in order to avoid dangerous rapids, or to continue their route west on another river. After a hard journey of 1,500 miles (2,400 km), the Frenchmen reached their goal. Along St. Marys River, which connects Lake Huron and Lake Superior, stood a settlement of Chippewa Indian huts and the cabins of a few dozen French traders. At this place, called "the Sault" (pronounced "soo"), Marquette was to establish a new mission.

Brother Louis and his two helpers immediately started work on the mission of Sault Sainte Marie. They chopped down trees with axes and built a log house, a chapel, and storage barns. Around these buildings they erected a protective wall of 12-foot (3.7-meter) cedar posts so the mission could also serve as a fort.

While his assistants did this work, Father Marquette preached to the local Chippewa. They listened respectfully to his sermons and welcomed the blackrobed priest into their huts to nurse sick children and to comfort the elderly. When Indians from other nations such as the Miami, Cree, and Illinois arrived at the St. Marys River to fish, Marquette spoke to them as well. He learned new words and sign language so he could preach to as many different tribes as possible.

Portaging a canoe over land

In the spring of 1669, two gray-haired priests, Father Claude Allouez and Father Claude Dablon, arrived at Sault Sainte Marie. Marquette hurried to the riverbank to greet them and soon learned the latest news. The Jesuits had chosen Father Dablon to serve as the religious superior of the entire Great Lakes region. He would use the mission of Sault Sainte Marie as his headquarters. At the same time, Father Allouez would find sites for new missions. Father Marquette's new duty was to replace Father Allouez at the mission of Saint Esprit on the southern shore of Lake Superior.

Thirty-two-year-old Father Marquette wished he could explore new lands like Father Allouez. He was a dutiful Jesuit, however, and he cheerfully accepted his assignment. In August 1669, he set forth with Indian friends on his long westward journey. Even summer weather was cold at this northern latitude. Crossing along the shore of Lake Superior, icy waves splashed into their canoes and freezing winds blew into their faces. At last the men reached the mission of Saint Esprit at Chequamegon Bay. ". . . after a voyage of a month amid snow and ice, which blocked our passage," Marquette wrote, "and amid almost constant dangers of death . . . I arrived here on the thirteenth of September. . . ."

The Ottawa and Huron Indians of Chequamegon Bay welcomed the blackrobe. Marquette immediately visited their scattered villages to nurse the sick and preach his faith. He lived among these people for a full year. In the spring he fished with them, and in the fall he joined their deer hunts. On snowy winter nights they sat together cross-legged in front of the mission fireplace.

The peace at Saint Esprit was broken in the spring of 1671, when bands of Sioux Indians began raiding

Icy Lake Superior

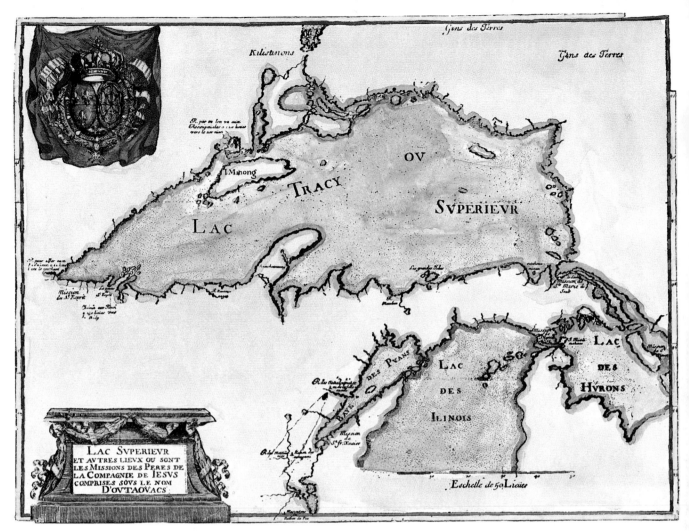

A Jesuit map of Lake Superior

the area. Father Marquette anxiously helped his flock of Christian Indians load their canoes. Paddling eastward he led these trusting natives in search of safety.

The fleeing Ottawas found a home on Manitoulin Island near Sault Sainte Marie. Marquette settled the Huron refugees at Michilimackinac, near the Mackinac Strait, which separated Lake Huron and Lake Michigan. In September 1671, he started work on a new mission called Saint Ignace. About 380 Huron and several families of Ottawa helped him build a mission house, chapel, and village cabins. Together they cut down trees and erected a high wall around the mission to protect against Sioux attack.

St. Ignace proved a fine place for a settlement. During the summer of 1672 the Indians planted their crops and watched them grow in the rich, dark soil. In the fall they collected great baskets of corn, squash, and other vegetables. In happy harvest celebrations called the "Feasts of the Squash," they made Father Marquette the guest of honor. Afterwards the dedicated priest led them all in singing hymns of thanks.

On the afternoon of December 8, 1672, several Huron children ran to the mission in search of Marquette. They had seen a canoe approaching off the point. The priest walked down the path from the mission to the water's edge. The canoe reached shore, and a stocky young Frenchman stepped onto the sandy beach. Marquette recognized him as the fur trader Louis Jolliet. The priest

Marquette joins Jolliet's group of explorers at St. Ignace.

welcomed the weary traveler. They soon sat together before a warm fire in the mission, and Marquette eagerly asked for the latest news.

Jolliet unwrapped an oilskin package. Inside lay a parchment document, which Jolliet unrolled and read aloud. It was an official commission appointing Jolliet to lead an expedition to explore the great river of the west. Marquette warmly congratulated Jolliet on his appointment. With a smile, Jolliet next presented the priest with a sealed letter from the Jesuit superior Father Dablon. The contents of this letter would change Jacques Marquette's life forever. After scanning the lines, he looked up with delighted eyes. When Jolliet's men started their expedition in the spring, Marquette was ordered to travel with them.

Chapter 4
A Son of New France

The roaring waters of the St. Lawrence River flowed past the colonial settlement of Beaupre. There, in a house of thick log timbers, Louis Jolliet was born in the summer of 1645. On September 21, Jean Jolliet and Marie d'Abancourt Jolliet bundled up their infant son and carried him out into the sunlight. Together they walked the path that led several miles upriver to Quebec. Quebec's parish priests were using the log and stone House of the One Hundred Associates as a temporary church. In a second-floor room of this fur company building, a priest touched a drop of holy oil on the baby's forehead and christened him.

The House of One Hundred Associates controlled the entire fur trade in New France. Like many colonists, Jean Jolliet worked for the company. He was a skilled wheelwright and wagonmaker. He used sharp saw blades, chisels, and mallets to fashion wooden wheels for handcarts. (In those early colonial days there was no need to build horse-drawn wagons. There were no horses in the entire colony until the first one was brought over from France in 1647.)

As the child Louis grew, he crawled about the Jolliet house and played with younger sister Marie and baby brother Zacharie. Louis also had an older brother named Adrien. When Adrien raced with his friends along the muddy streets of Beaupre, Louis tried to join in the fun. On some days Louis held onto his mother's skirt and followed her to the marketplace. He saw bearded backwoodsmen carrying venison and wild turkeys for sale. He stared with wide eyes at the peaceful Indians selling bright orange pumpkins and yellow squashes. At the family fireside, Louis listened with close attention when his father gossiped with neighborhood friends. He heard exciting tales about fur trappers and forest pioneers. He trembled at the news of bloody Iroquois Indian attacks south of the St. Lawrence River.

Jean Jolliet died in 1651 after a long illness. In New France, where men greatly outnumbered women, Marie Jolliet did not remain a widow very long. After a period of respectful mourning, a colonist named Geoffroy Guillot began calling upon her, and they were married within a year.

Geoffroy Guillot earned a prosperous living as a Quebec trader. He owned a stone house in the lower town, as well as property on the Ile d'Orleans, a nearby island in the St. Lawrence River. Six-year-old Louis loved exploring the woods and hills of Ile d'Orleans. Jesuit priests recently had settled 600 Huron refugees on the island to protect them from the Iroquois. Louis often visited the Huron village. He wandered among the Indian huts, observed how they lived, and sometimes shared their meals. As time passed, the bright young boy learned many words of the Huron language.

Geoffroy Guillot could afford to provide his stepchildren with a proper education. At about the age of nine,

Les Cinq Nations Iroquoises

Lac Ontario ou des Iroquois

A French map of Lake Ontario and the Iroquois Country

Louis Jolliet began studying at the Jesuit college in Quebec. He worked on arithmetic problems, practiced his writing skills, and learned Latin. Perhaps most of all he enjoyed drawing. With pens and pencils he carefully sketched Quebec street scenes and pictures of the ships in the harbor. At the age of thirteen Louis drew a map of the St. Lawrence River. It showed everything he knew about the course of the river, but he wished to learn much more.

During 1658, Louis's seventeen-year-old brother, Adrien Jolliet, worked at the Guillot fur warehouse at Three Rivers. One June morning, Adrien and two other boys hiked into the forest, but strayed too far into the woods. From behind the trees stepped a band of Iroquois Indians with painted faces. The boys were kidnapped.

All summer long Louis worried about his missing brother. He feared the Iroquois might torture and kill Adrien. But after three agonizing months, wonderful news reached Quebec. Adrien and one of the other boys had been set free. Louis hurried west to Three Rivers for a reunion with his brother. Louis was enthralled as he listened to Adrien's gripping tale of life among the Iroquois. For many months, thoughts of Adrien's brave adventure often kept Louis awake at night.

Louis resumed his studies at the Jesuit college in the fall. As a scholar he could debate fine points of philosophy and recite classical writings in Greek. Father Claude Dablon was a skilled musician and taught several instruments. During the next years Louis proved his talent as a music student. The other boys crowded close and sang while Louis played harpsichord. At chapel services he often performed on the flute or the trumpet.

In 1662, at the age of seventeen, Louis chose to study for the Jesuit priesthood. He dressed in the robe of an apprentice priest and continued advanced studies. Returning from a visit to France, Bishop Francois Laval brought back a grand pipe organ for the Quebec cathedral. On Christmas Eve 1664, it was probably Louis Jolliet who played this organ for the first time. Pulling the stops and pressing the pedals, he flooded the cathedral with the rumbling notes of majestic hymns.

Stories of the West, however, still excited Louis's imagination. He felt increasingly torn between his love of the church and his personal ambitions. The mysteries and adventures of Canada's backwoods seemed to beckon him. During the summer of 1667, he spoke privately with Bishop Laval. With gentle understanding the bishop agreed to release the young man from his holy vows to the Jesuits.

In the fall of 1667, twenty-two-year-old Louis Jolliet dressed in a new suit of clothes and boarded a ship in Quebec harbor. Around him busy sailors raised the canvas sails. The helmsman soon steered downriver and into the Atlantic, bound for France. It is unknown exactly why Jolliet made this journey to France. Bishop Laval loaned him the money for the trip, and perhaps Louis carried out an errand for the bishop. The ship rocked forward through the green Atlantic waves during the two-and-a-half-month crossing and eventually docked at the French port of La Rochelle. Seated in a bouncing coach, Jolliet stared with fascination at the French countryside before him. The clatter of horse hooves on cobblestones finally announced his arrival in Paris.

Quebec Harbor

Surely the crowded streets, ancient houses, and grand palaces of the French capital impressed Jolliet. This was his mother country, yet it was the first time in his life he had visited. During his stay in Paris it is possible Jolliet improved his youthful mapmaking skills. A Monsieur Franquelin sometimes taught promising pupils hydrography—the study of seas, lakes, rivers, and other bodies of water. Such a course would have interested a talented young man like Jolliet. In addition, Bishop Laval would have recognized the value of having a skilled hydrographer in New France.

Louis Jolliet finished his business in France by August 1668. Once again he leaned upon a deck rail and watched the ocean waves as he sailed home. The ship at last coasted up the St. Lawrence River and anchored in Quebec harbor. At the family townhouse, Louis's mother looked up from her work and saw her son stepping through the doorway. After they hugged in happy reunion, Louis announced his plans for his future. Adrien and Zacharie Jolliet had gone west to work in the fur trade, and Louis intended to join them.

Once again Jolliet relied on the good will of Bishop Laval. The kindly bishop loaned him enough money to get started as a trader. On October 9, 1668, Louis purchased from a Quebec merchant two guns, two pistols, a hat, woolen material to be sewn into clothes, and two pair of shoes. He also bought items he could use for trading with the Indians: beads, bells, twenty-four hatchets, bolts of coarse cloth and canvas, and forty pounds of tobacco.

Adrien Jolliet owned a fur warehouse at the settlement of Cap-de-la-Madeleine near Three Rivers, where Zacharie Jolliet worked as well. At the riverside Louis Jolliet soon unloaded his stock of trade goods and found the cabin where Adrien lived with his wife and children. Louis and Adrien had not seen one another in a long time. Before the warmth of the cabin fireplace the two brothers smoked pipes and talked. Louis told marvelous stories of France and Paris. Adrien filled his brother's ears with tales of his trading journeys in the wilderness. By the flickering firelight Louis gazed at his older brother with admiration.

The fur trade kept Louis Jolliet busy during the next months. Ottawas, Hurons, and other Indians paddled their canoes to Cap-de-la-Madeleine with bundles of lustrous beaver pelts. At his brother's warehouse, Louis examined the furs and offered his best prices. The Jolliet brothers worked well together, but in the spring of 1669 their partnership was interrupted.

Indians bring beaver skins to French fur traders.

In Quebec Jean-Baptiste Talon served as intendant, the colonial officer second only to the governor. The success of New France's economy greatly concerned this man of intelligence and energy. In the spring of 1667, rumors had reached Talon that valuable copper ore might be found along the western shores of Lake Superior. Talon searched for a brave man to send west to investigate. Adrien Jolliet had already proven himself a bold explorer. He spoke several Indian languages and was known to be trustworthy. Talon chose Adrien Jolliet to scout for the copper mines.

Adrien set off on his journey in July 1669. He successfully reached the western shores of Lake Superior, but he found little evidence of copper mines. At summer's end he paddled for home, this time accompanied by a friendly Iroquois. On September 24, 1669, the two men landed along the western shore of Lake Ontario. At least seven other canoes already lay in a row on the beach. They belonged to an exploring expedition led by Rene Robert Cavelier, Sieur de La Salle. Intendant Talon had sent La Salle to search for the Big River. (La Salle, many years later, was one of the first Europeans to reach the Mississippi.) In camp that night Adrien offered La Salle traveling advice, but the proud and boastful explorer barely listened.

The next morning Adrien and his Iroquois companion continued eastward. They were never seen again. Nobody knows exactly what happened, but all trace of Adrien Jolliet disappeared.

The loss of his admired brother deeply saddened Louis Jolliet. To help support Adrien's widow and children, Louis vowed to carry on the fur trading business. Jolliet journeyed west with several business partners in the summer of 1670. At the mission of Sault

Sainte Marie the men unloaded their canoes. In a clearing Jolliet set up a forge complete with bellows and heavy anvil. The men built a log cabin and stacked their barrels and packs of trade goods inside. During the next two years Jolliet worked hard at his new frontier trading post. When passing voyagers spoke of the search for the western copper mines, Jolliet listened with interest. Continuing rumors of the Big River excited him even more. The boy who loved mapmaking had grown into a man who still wished to explore.

In Quebec, Intendant Talon paced in his office. By the summer of 1672, La Salle had not returned from his unsuccessful western expedition. Talon felt sure the territory beyond the western frontier held riches guaranteed to help New France. Perhaps the fabled Big River was even a passageway leading to China and Japan. Talon yearned to find out for sure.

Word reached Louis Jolliet that the intendant wished to speak with him. The fur trader traveled to Quebec and in time was announced at the door of the governor's palace. Talon stood before him in a great curled wig and a handsome long coat trimmed with golden thread and shining buttons. Talon knew of Jolliet's Jesuit education and his skills as a mapmaker. He was aware that Louis had followed his brother Adrien into the fur trade. Talon felt he could trust this Jolliet as well, so he presented his plan. Would Jolliet be willing to command a new western expedition to find the Big River? As payment, the government would grant him and his partners trading rights in whatever new territories he explored. Jolliet's eyes blazed with excitement as he happily accepted. He suddenly felt certain that success and glory awaited him on the banks of the swirling Mississippi.

Jean Baptiste Talon

Chapter 5
"He is Well Suited for This Sort of Discovery"

Tadou sac

La grande.R

71

72

ÇA

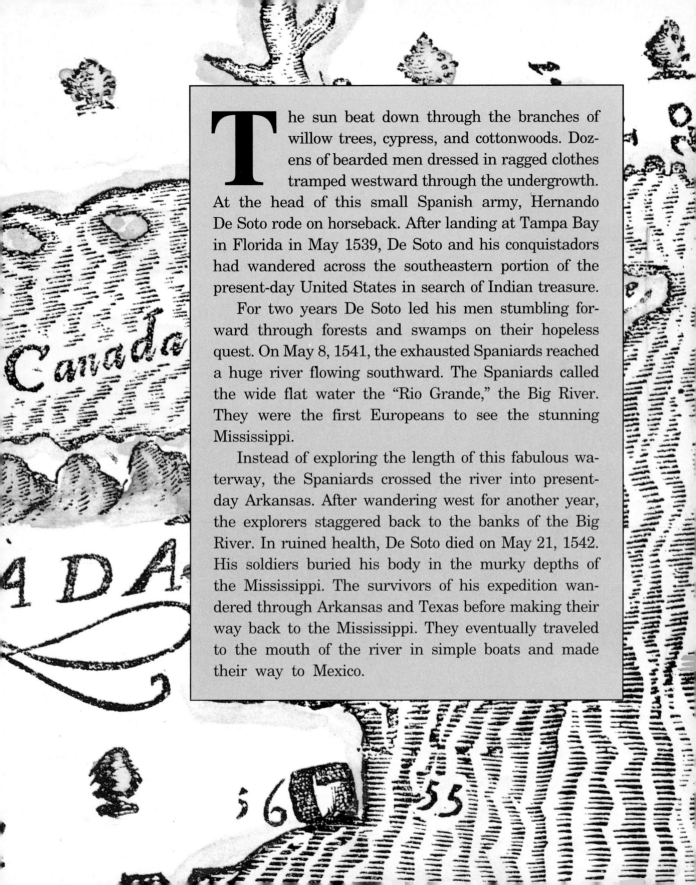

The sun beat down through the branches of willow trees, cypress, and cottonwoods. Dozens of bearded men dressed in ragged clothes tramped westward through the undergrowth. At the head of this small Spanish army, Hernando De Soto rode on horseback. After landing at Tampa Bay in Florida in May 1539, De Soto and his conquistadors had wandered across the southeastern portion of the present-day United States in search of Indian treasure.

For two years De Soto led his men stumbling forward through forests and swamps on their hopeless quest. On May 8, 1541, the exhausted Spaniards reached a huge river flowing southward. The Spaniards called the wide flat water the "Rio Grande," the Big River. They were the first Europeans to see the stunning Mississippi.

Instead of exploring the length of this fabulous waterway, the Spaniards crossed the river into present-day Arkansas. After wandering west for another year, the explorers staggered back to the banks of the Big River. In ruined health, De Soto died on May 21, 1542. His soldiers buried his body in the murky depths of the Mississippi. The survivors of his expedition wandered through Arkansas and Texas before making their way back to the Mississippi. They eventually traveled to the mouth of the river in simple boats and made their way to Mexico.

Hernando de Soto

The discovery of the Mississippi represented by far the greatest success of De Soto's expedition. Spain later claimed the entire river as part of its colonial empire in North America. Yet its length remained unexplored.

During the next century, French-Canadian fur traders pushed farther and farther west, following the St. Lawrence River and the rivers that flowed into the Great Lakes. At the same time, English colonists established settlements on the Atlantic coast. France and England clearly intended to make claims in North America, as well as Spain.

Although many Indian tribes had mapped their territories, the complete map of the continent remained a mystery to the European newcomers. In the 1630s the French hoped the Great Lakes provided a water route to Asia. In 1634, explorer Jean Nicolet became the first European to enter Lake Michigan. Crossing the wide lake, he reached Green Bay on the shores of present-day Wisconsin. Other Frenchmen eventually visited this distant northwest region. Jesuit missionary Claude Allouez landed among the Potawatomie and Sauk Indians of Green Bay in December 1669. The next spring, Allouez ventured even farther, paddling his canoe up the Fox River. There he met Indians of the Maskouten and Miami nations. Allouez observed how they lived and learned what he could about the region. "These people," he later revealed, "are settled in a very attractive place where beautiful plains and fields meet the eye as far as one can see. Their river leads by a six days' voyage to a great river named Messi-Sipi."

Other Indians also spoke of the Mississippi. While working at Sault Sainte Marie in 1669, Jacques Marquette heard one story. A Shawnee prisoner of the Ottawas described a great river that flowed into the

"South Sea." The river lay five days' distance from his home village. Later that year at Saint Esprit, the Ottawas released a young captive Illinois Indian into Father Marquette's care. During many cold winter evenings the priest sat with the Illinois youth slowly learning his native language. The Illinois boy told Marquette many things about his homeland to the south. The boy claimed a great river flowed from north to south through the rolling prairies.

Rumors of the Mississippi filtered back to Quebec and onward to France. Some European geographers guessed that the Mississippi and the Spanish Rio Grande (a thousand miles [1,600 km] to the south) might be the same powerful river. Intendant Talon quickly recognized the value of spreading French influence to such a river. Claim to the natural resources of the upper Mississippi would strengthen the economy of New France.

Louis Jolliet accepted the commission offered to him by Intendant Talon in 1672. "He is well suited for this sort of discovery . . ." agreed the Count de Frontenac, the governor of New France. Intendant Talon granted Jolliet a royal license to act as an agent of the French government.

"They were not mistaken in the choice they made of Sieur Jolyet," Father Claude Dablon, now the Jesuit superior in Quebec, soon declared, "For he is a young man, born in this country, who . . . has experience and Knows the Languages spoken in the Country of the Outaouacs [Ottawas]. . . ." To spread the Roman Catholic faith, Father Dablon urged that a Jesuit priest familiar with exploring should also join the expedition. Jolliet, who knew many of the Jesuits, wondered which priest Father Dablon would choose.

Father Marquette

In the meantime Jolliet organized the expedition. His younger brother Zacharie joined in the enterprise, and several other old trading partners and fur trappers wished to take part as well. On October 1, 1672, the men crowded into a Quebec house to sign their contract. "Before Gilles Rageot, notary," declared the document, ". . . were present . . . Louis Jolliet, Francois Chavigny . . . Zacharie Jolliet, Jean Plattier, Pierre Moreau, Jacques Largillier, Jean Tiberge . . . who of their own free will have entered into partnership and society to make together the voyage to the Ottawa country [to] trade with the Indians as profitably as possible. . . ."

On October 2, 1672, the partners pushed their loaded canoes into the shallow water of the St. Lawrence and

Louis Jolliet

jumped aboard. They started upriver on their long journey, paddling with slow, rhythmic strokes. The Frenchmen ascended the Ottawa River, crossed Lake Nipissing and Georgian Bay, and by the end of autumn landed at Sault Sainte Marie. While his partners reopened the Jolliet trading post, Louis Jolliet paddled 70 miles (113 km) south to the mission of St. Ignace at Michilimackinac.

Chilling winds whipped the dark waters at the western edge of Lake Huron. On December 8, Jolliet swung his canoe ashore at St. Ignace. Father Marquette welcomed every visitor to his mission with warmth and kindness. When Jolliet handed the priest the letter from Father Dablon, however, Marquette's eyes lit up with special happiness. The letter crackled in his trembling hands as he read it several times. Marquette was the Jesuit priest chosen to join Jolliet's expedition into the mysterious regions of the Mississippi.

Twenty-seven-year-old Jacques Marquette and thirty-five-year-old Louis Jolliet already knew one another. Years earlier Marquette had heard Jolliet play the organ at the Cathedral of Quebec. Marquette had later visited the mission at Sault Sainte Marie when Jolliet first ran his trading post there. The two men shared much in common and they trusted one another.

During the next days they excitedly discussed their project. On paper they sketched a rough map, drawing the Mississippi where they guessed it could be found. The two men agreed that the most promising travel route would be the one pioneered by Father Allouez beyond Green Bay. Before the icy winter weather set in, Jolliet left St. Ignace and paddled back to Sault Sainte Marie. He promised to return with his partners in the spring and pick up Marquette.

Throughout the winter months, thick ice clogged the rivers and covered the lakes. Piles of snow drifted higher and higher. Indians and Frenchmen remained in their snug cabins as much as possible. At last, the spring thaw arrived, and the Frenchmen at Sault Sainte Marie heard the loud crack of ice breaking on the St. Marys River.

Jolliet and his partners examined their two canoes to see that wooden struts and birchbark coverings had survived the winter storms. They arranged their baggage into firm bundles and packed everything aboard. It was decided that Zacharie Jolliet would remain at the trading post to look out for business there. For an unknown reason Francois Chavigny also probably stayed behind. On a bright day in May 1673, Louis Jolliet, Jean Tiberge, Jacques Largillier, Pierre Moreau, Jean Plattier, and a new sixth man (possibly named Pierre Porteret) shoved off for St. Ignace.

Across blue water the men paddled to the point of land that separated Lake Huron and Lake Michigan. Father Marquette waited ashore, eager to join them. For a few days the men rested at St. Ignace and reviewed their final plans. Jolliet showed the priest his compass for finding directions and another instrument, an astrolabe, which measured latitudes with the help of the sun. The explorers again checked their bundles to see that their gunpowder was dry and their trading goods were in order. "We were not long in preparing all our Equipment," Father Marquette later explained, "although we were about to Begin a voyage, the duration of which we could not foresee."

On the morning of May 17, 1673, everything seemed ready. While the Indians of St. Ignace watched, the men stepped into the cold water and climbed aboard the two canoes. Soon the adventurers paddled away on their voyage of discovery. The canoes glided westward along the shoreline of Lake Michigan. One kneeling man paddled at the bow of each canoe while another paddled and steered from his position at the stern. The third man in each canoe rested, waiting for his turn with a paddle. Father Marquette, however, always sat at the middle of one canoe. The others, out of respect for the priest, had agreed that Marquette should do no paddling work.

Overhead, waterbirds whirled high among the clouds. Through the shoreline trees, breezes carried the sweet smells of spring across the water. The voyagers traveled about 30 miles (48 km) each day. Each night they

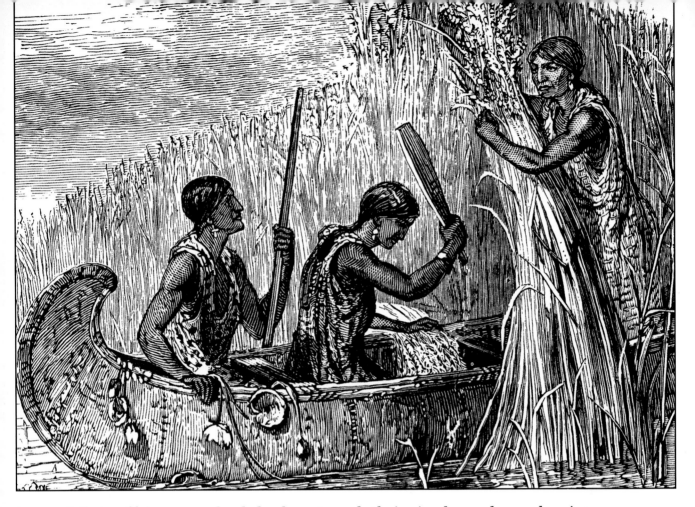

Gathering wild rice

landed ashore to cook their simple meals, smoke pipes, and roll into their blankets for sleep. The explorers entered Green Bay after several days, and early in June they reached the Menominee River.

The huts of Menominee Indians stood near the mouth of the river. The friendly Indians lined the shore and welcomed the Frenchmen as their canoes coasted close. These Menominee were also called the Wild Rice Indians. The greatest part of their diet consisted of the wild rice that grew abundantly in the region. At harvest time each September, the Menominee paddled through the rice marshes, shaking the stems over their canoes. The ripe rice grains separated and fell, filling the canoes like great grain baskets. In this easy manner the Menominee obtained their yearly rice supply.

Marquette and Jolliet explained that they were on their way to find the Big River, and the Menominee delivered their warnings of the many dangers that lay ahead: the unfriendly Indians tribes that populated the riverbanks; the terrible monsters that lurked beneath the water; the river demon that barred travelers and swallowed men and their canoes together. They even told the Frenchmen that at the mouth of the river, the sun blazed so hot it burned men to death.

"I thanked them for the good advice," recalled Marquette, but he and Jolliet were pledged to go forward with their mission.

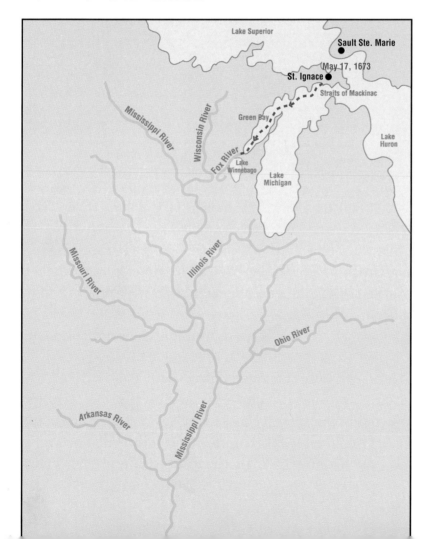

A placid portion of the Fox River

The Menominee waved good-bye as the explorers soon paddled onward down Green Bay. The canoes glided southward to the mouth of the Fox River. The Jesuit mission of Saint Francis-Xavier stood here. A single crude cabin, it was the most distant French settlement into the territory. Marquette and Jolliet stopped briefly and exchanged news with Father Claude Allouez. The old priest gave his blessings to the men and wished them success in fulfilling their difficult task.

The explorers followed the route of the Fox River inland. At first the river flowed with glassy calmness. Soon, however, it changed dramatically. ". . . after ascending the river a short distance," Father Marquette later exclaimed, "it becomes very difficult of passage, on account of both the Currents and the sharp

Rocks. . . ." At each of five dangerous rapids the voyagers paddled to shore and unloaded the packs from the canoes. They then dragged the empty canoes through the rapids. They stepped carefully among the pointed underwater rocks, choosing the shortest path to smooth water. After crossing each set of rapids, the men went back and lugged their gear over land and repacked the canoes.

Beyond the rapids, the Fox River widened into shallow Lake Winnebago. The canoes glided through marshes of reeds and smelly swamps. Following the current for 20 miles (32 km), the Frenchmen eventually found the southwestern entrance to the upper Fox River. Beyond lay the territory of the Maskouten Indian nation. For another 50 miles (80 km), the explorers paddled upstream. On June 7, the canoes rounded a bend in the river. On the distant shore stood the great Maskouten village. Jesuit priests had visited the town in the past but had not ventured any farther. "Here is the limit of the discoveries which the French have made," Jacques Marquette remarked in his journal.

The Maskouten chiefs welcomed the seven Frenchmen with formal speeches. They passed a long-stemmed pipe, called a calumet, filled with tobacco. The men smoked as a sign of peace and then enjoyed a feast.

After the feast, Louis Jolliet spoke to the chiefs. He told them that he was sent by the French government to explore new territory. He also explained that the "blackrobe," Father Marquette, was sent by God to spread the Roman Catholic faith. Jolliet asked the chiefs for help in finding the Mississippi. As a symbol of agreement the Maskoutens presented Marquette and Jolliet with a mat of woven reeds to serve as a bed during their journey.

Site of the Mascouten Indian village

A number of Miami Indians lived among the Maskoutens. On the morning of June 10, two skilled Miami guides joined the seven Frenchmen at the riverbank. As they prepared to depart, Marquette described the gathered crowd of Indians as " . . . [astonished] at the sight of seven Frenchmen, alone and in two Canoes, daring to undertake so extraordinary and so hazardous an Expedition."

The Maskouten shared the Menominees' fears of the unknown Mississippi. As they boarded their canoes, the Frenchmen likely felt more anxious than ever before. Beyond the Maskouten village lay lands never before seen by Europeans.

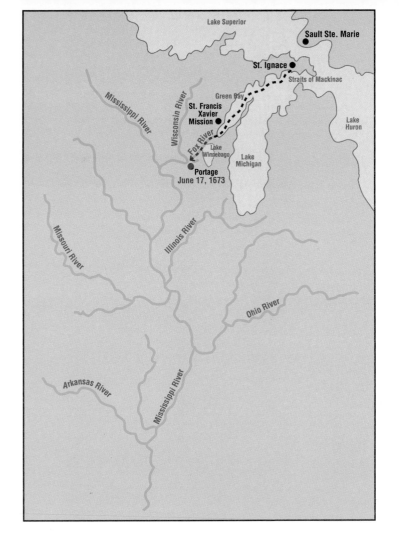

The Miami guides led the way, paddling their own canoe. Above the Maskouten village, the course of the Fox River twisted through a maze of swamps and small lakes. The three canoes glided among drooping willow trees, marshy alder thickets, and stands of cattails. About 10 miles (16 km) up the Fox River, the two Miamis suddenly steered for shore, signaling for the Frenchmen to follow. It was here that the Fox River and the Wisconsin River nearly touched (the present-day site of Portage, Wisconsin). The Fox River flowed east and the Wisconsin River flowed west. Marquette and Jolliet could only guess that the second river, the Wisconsin, drained into the Mississippi.

Portage, Wisconsin, where Marquette and Jolliet parted ways with their Indian guides and entered the Wisconsin River

The Miamis helped the Frenchmen unload their canoes. Four of the strongest men lifted the two canoes onto their shoulders. The others hefted packs and gear. They carried everything overland to the Wisconsin River. The men stepped slowly along the muddy trail under the weight of their heavy loads. Willow branches slapped at their faces. They stubbed their toes and tripped on roots. Father Marquette carefully counted every step of the way. After 2,700 paces (about 1.5 miles [2.5 km]), they reached the banks of the Wisconsin River.

The explorers lay the two canoes in the water and reloaded their supplies so the weight was balanced. The Miami guides would go no farther. They watched silently until the work was finished. Then the two Indians solemnly raised their hands in farewell and disappeared into the woods. ". . . they returned home," commented Father Marquette, "leaving us alone in this Unknown country, in the hands of providence." The French traders gathered around Father Marquette. They knelt together, and the Jesuit priest prayed for heavenly blessings. The Frenchmen boarded their canoes, pushed off with their paddles, and launched onto the Wisconsin River.

"Thus we left the Waters flowing to Quebec," explained Father Marquette, ". . . to float on Those that would thenceforward Take us through strange lands. . . ."

The Wisconsin River

Chapter 6
"How Beautiful the Sun Is, O Frenchman"

The River on which we embarked," Jacques Marquette wrote in his journal, ". . . is very wide. . . . full of Islands Covered with Vines. On the banks one sees fertile land . . . woods, prairies and Hills." The French explorers followed the current down the Wisconsin River. At first the canoes gently scraped over sandy shallows. Soon, however, the cold, brown water deepened and the birchbark boats coasted easily. Wispy willow thickets along the shore gradually gave way to groves of hardy walnut and oak trees.

At night around their campfires the seven men listened to the hooting of owls. In the day as they glided onward they spied beavers gnawing wood and deer bounding among meadow flowers. On the open prairies the voyagers saw herds of buffalo for the first time. They called these startling creatures "wild cattle" because they looked like giant, shaggy bulls and cows. Father Marquette counted one large herd of 400 animals eating the prairie grass, rolling in the dirt, and running with thundering hooves.

For seven days the explorers traveled the course of the Wisconsin. On the morning of June 17, 1673, the men followed the current as usual, dipping their paddles with easy strokes. A haze hung over the water as the two canoes passed a low island thickly covered with willow trees. Beyond the island they saw that the wide Wisconsin merged with an even greater river. It flowed from the north to the south and measured over a mile across. The Frenchmen gaped and grinned as they realized they had reached the Big River, the mighty Mississippi.

The two canoes coasted forward, letting the Mississippi current guide them. The men laughed aloud, let their hands trail in the deep dark water, and gave thanks for this proud moment of discovery. "Here we are then, on this so renowned River," wrote Father Marquette. With his astrolabe Jolliet measured their latitude and marked the historic spot on his map.

The explorers steered their canoes down the Mississippi. On the right riverbank, high rocky bluffs jutted into the sky, while to the left, dense woodlands filled the horizon. Songbirds sat in the tree branches, while ducks and herons nested in the marshy coves. The smooth river current flowed in a course that looped lazily back and forth with broad twists and turns; but its general direction always carried the explorers farther south. The voyagers paddled around dead trees and broken branches floating in the water. Long, narrow islands sometimes split the river into channels for a mile or two, but the water always drew together again. The countryside beside them eventually widened into open prairies. "There are hardly any woods or mountains," Father Marquette noted. "The islands are more beautiful, and are Covered with finer trees."

During these first few days of travel, life on the Mississippi seemed quite peaceful—except when the Frenchmen encountered strange river animals. "From time to time," exclaimed Marquette, "we came upon monstrous fish, one of which struck our Canoe with such violence that I Thought it was a great tree, about to break the Canoe to pieces." The fish that accidentally rammed Marquette's canoe was probably a tiger-catfish. It is no longer found in the Mississippi, but in past years, river fishermen sometimes hooked tiger-catfish weighing up to one hundred pounds.

The explorers threw fishing nets into the water and sometimes trapped sturgeon for extra food. One day, Pierre Porteret shouted at the sight of his strange catch. A large, struggling fish nearly yanked the net from his hands. Its smooth, scaleless skin glistened in the sunlight. The shape of its snout was long and flat. The unusual fish was probably a paddle-billed catfish.

Buffaloes grazing near the riverbanks continued to amaze the voyagers. One day while stopping on shore they shot one down. Father Marquette joined the others in examining the dead animal. Three men lifting together could barely budge the shaggy beast. "The head is very large," described Marquette. "The forehead is flat, and a foot and a half Wide between the Horns. . . . The whole of the head, the Neck and a portion of the Shoulders, are Covered with a thick Mane Like That of horses. . . . The remainder of the Body is covered with a heavy coat of curly hair, almost Like That of our sheep, but much stronger and thicker."

In the seventeenth century, buffalo still populated North America in great numbers.

Day after day the gentle river current drew the explorers farther southward. "We continued to advance," remarked Father Marquette, "but, As we knew not whither we were going . . . we kept well on our guard." Each evening the men paddled to shore and cooked a hasty meal over a small fire. As soon as they finished eating they stamped out the fire and buried smoking sticks, fish bones, and other evidence of their presence. ". . . we . . . pass the night in our Canoes," reported Marquette, "which we anchor in the river at some distance from the shore. This does not prevent us from always posting one of the party as a sentinel, for fear of a surprise."

The guard aboard the canoes relaxed as the first rays of morning sunshine cracked through the shoreline trees. The waking Frenchmen yawned and stretched and washed their faces in the cool river water. After a brief breakfast and probably a prayer offered by their Jesuit priest, the men raised their anchors and took up their paddles. The canoes sliced through the water. Each paddlestroke made the water gurgle. Splashing drops of water sparkled in the light. The paddling Frenchmen remained crouched at the front and rear of each canoe in half-kneeling positions. The muscles in their shoulders and arms had grown hard and strong. Their hands grew callused from gripping the wooden paddles. The sun reflected on the water's surface and tanned their faces.

For a full week, the explorers floated down the Mississippi without seeing any sign of Indians, but on June 25, they discovered footprints in a muddy riverbank. A narrow trail led from the river up a slope among the willow trees. Regardless of the danger, Marquette and Jolliet agreed they should explore this trail. Both

The journey continues down the Mississippi.

men were determined to learn what they could about the Indians of the region. "We therefore left our two Canoes under the guard of our people," recalled Marquette, "strictly charging them not to allow themselves to be surprised."

Jolliet slung a small bag of trade goods over his shoulder. Father Marquette drew up the hem of his long black robe to keep from tripping. The five others watched from the canoes as these two brave men disappeared into the willow grove. The priest and the trader stepped silently along the trail and soon entered the open prairie. They followed the path for several hours before they saw an Indian village. It stood in the

Marquette approaches the Illinois Indians for the first time.

distance on a ridge beside a river. For a moment they held their breath. Then, full of prayers and courage, they continued forward.

They approached so close to the village they could hear the Indians talking. "We therefore Decided," Marquette later explained, "that it was time to reveal ourselves. This We did by Shouting with all Our energy, and stopped without advancing farther." The sudden yelling brought men, women, and children scrambling out of their cabins. While dogs barked, these natives stared at their strange visitors with complete surprise. Marquette and Jolliet waited tensely, wondering if they would be greeted as friends or enemies.

Marquette and Jolliet are greeted by the Illinois.

Four old men stepped forward from the throng of Indians. Two of these village elders carried long tobacco pipes, finely carved and adorned with feathers. As they advanced, they raised the pipes to the sun. They reached the two white men and halted. Marquette and Jolliet guessed that they were friendly. Father Marquette cleared his throat. In the Illinois language he asked them who they were.

Greatly impressed, the four elders replied that they were Illinois Indians of the group called the Peoria. ". . . as a token of peace," Marquette recalled, "they offered us their pipes to smoke. . . . These pipes for smoking tobacco are called in This country Calumets." Marquette and Jolliet puffed on the pipes and then the elders invited them to enter the village. The villagers stared with keen curiosity as the priest and the trader walked among the bark-covered cabins. These Illinois probably had heard of Frenchmen but had never seen any. Marquette and Jolliet were led to the cabin of the village chieftain. The old man stood naked in his cabin doorway with his arms lifted toward the sun.

"How beautiful the sun is, O Frenchmen," exclaimed the aged chief in greeting, "when thou comest to visit us! All our village awaits thee, and thou shalt enter all our Cabins in peace."

The chieftain motioned them inside. Sitting cross-legged, Marquette and Jolliet again puffed on a calumet. From the crowded doorway villagers peered through the tobacco smoke for a glimpse of the foreigners.

Messengers spread the news quickly among the villages, and the chief of all the region's Illinois invited the Frenchmen to visit. Marquette and Jolliet started immediately, followed along the route by hundreds of the Illinois. "For all those people," explained Marquette, "who had never seen any Frenchmen among Them, could not cease looking at us. They Lay on The grass along the road; they preceded us, and then retraced their steps to come and see us Again. All this was done noiselessly, and with marks of great respect for us."

Marquette and Jolliet reached a village of some 300 cabins. With the greetings of the great chief of the Illinois came more peace pipe smoking. Inside the chief's large cabin the two explorers soon sat with the gathered leaders of the village. Jolliet opened the bag he carried and Father Marquette handed out several presents. At the same time Marquette explained the reasons for their visit. Ever mindful of his religious mission, he first revealed his desire to spread the word of God. Then he explained their plan to paddle down the Mississippi to the sea. He asked the Illinois for information about the river's course and the Indian nations who lived along it.

The Illinois chief rose and put his hand upon the shoulder of a nearby Indian boy. "I thank thee, Blackgown, and thee O Frenchman," he declared to Marquette and Jolliet, "for having taken so much trouble to come to visit us. Never has the earth been so beautiful, or the sun so bright as today; never has our river been so calm, or so clear of rocks, which your canoes have removed in passing; never has our tobacco tasted so good, or our corn appeared so fine, as we now see them. Here is my son, whom I give thee to show thee my heart."

He presented the young boy, perhaps nine years old, to Jolliet to accompany the Frenchmen on their journey. To Marquette he made the gift of a handsome, long-stemmed calumet with a polished gray pipestone. The chief knew nothing of the Mississippi or the Indians who lived to the south. The Illinois had lived in the region only a short time. The chief feared that many dangers awaited the Frenchmen. As a symbol of peace, he hoped the calumet would protect the explorers wherever they traveled.

A great feast followed this council meeting. Servants first brought in a wooden platter piled with sagamite, a mush of boiled Indian corn, seasoned with fat. "The

Master of Ceremonies filled a Spoon with sagamite three or 4 times, and put it to my mouth As if I were a little Child," remembered Marquette with astonishment. "He did the same with Monsieur Jollyet." During the meal's second course, the Master of Ceremonies fed the two Frenchmen cooked fish with his fingers, often blowing on it to cool it. Politely Marquette and Jolliet refused to eat any of the offered third course, roasted dog. The final fourth course was wild ox meat.

That night Marquette and Jolliet slept in the chief's cabin as honored guests. The next day they walked back across the prairie. Curious Illinois villagers crowded beside them on the trail. These Indians lined the Mississippi riverbank as the priest and the trader rejoined their five French comrades. Marquette and Jolliet took their seats aboard the canoes. The Illinois chief insisted that Jolliet take his son with him. Quietly the boy obeyed and climbed aboard as well. The boy eventually became a kind of foster son to Jolliet and the explorers. In the days that followed he would share in all of the unfolding wonders of the Mississippi River.

Chapter 7
The Value of a Calumet

"We take leave of our Illinois at the end of June, about three o'clock in the afternoon," wrote Father Marquette in his journal. "We embark in the sight of all the people, who admire our little canoes, for they have never seen any like them." The French explorers pushed out into the river current and glided away to the south.

During the next days the voyagers followed the lazy course of the Mississippi in comfort. They listened to the twittering birds and munched on mulberries and nuts that they picked during rests ashore. The Menominees and the Illinois both had warned of terrible river demons, and one day early in July, the dreaded monsters suddenly appeared. The explorers gasped at the sight of two weird pictures painted in green, red, and black high upon the east riverbank cliffs.

"While Skirting some rocks," Marquette exclaimed, ". . . We saw . . . two painted monsters which at first made Us afraid, and upon which the boldest savages dare not Long rest their eyes. They are as large As a calf; they have Horns on their heads Like those of deer, a horrible . . . face somewhat like a man's, a body Covered with scales, and so long a tail that it winds all around the Body, passing above the head and going back between the legs, ending in a Fish's tail." These rock pictures glared from the cliffs near present-day Alton, Illinois, for many years.

The explorers talked about the startling paintings as their canoes coasted ahead. It seemed these painted monsters were intended as a warning that danger awaited river travelers and they should go no farther. The Frenchmen soon discovered the danger. Just another 12 miles (20 km) downstream, a torrential roar filled their ears. From the northwest, a tremendous stream of muddy water poured forth. The furious current swept along logs, branches, and uprooted trees. It joined the Mississippi and turned the calm green water wild and brown. This was the great Missouri River spilling its spring floodwaters into the Mississippi. "I have seen nothing more dreadful," Marquette later declared. The surprised explorers gripped their paddles as the swirling current spun the canoes along. With aching strokes the men managed to stay in the smoother water near the Mississippi's eastern riverbank.

The boats slipped past the river junction undamaged, but within a few hours, they entered a raging set of rapids (later named the "Chain of Rocks"). With quick reflexes, the tired voyagers steered left and right avoiding danger. The canoes finally passed the last rock and the river grew calm once more.

Junction of the Missouri and Mississippi Rivers

The explorers continued to follow the river's snaking course southward. In another few days the beautiful Ohio River joined the Mississippi from the east. With his astrolabe, Jolliet calculated this location as 36 degrees north latitude. The green waters of the Ohio mixed and churned with the muddied Mississippi. The Big River became even bigger and more impressive.

The explorers met new challenges every day. Sometimes they steered away from floating driftwood that threatened to ram the soft sides of the canoes. At other times paddlers spotted sharp snags just below the surface of the water. These tree branches, stuck in the river mud, could easily tear the bottom out of a canoe. The Frenchmen paddled ahead, always on the lookout for such hidden dangers. On calm days the men sometimes put up small masts and canvas sails. While they relaxed, gentle breezes carried them along their course.

The climate changed as the canoes passed farther southward. "Here we Began to see Canes, or large reeds," remarked Marquette, "which grow on the bank of the river; their color is a very pleasing green." The summer sun burned hotter every day. The men mopped their sweating brows and cooled sunburned arms and faces with handfuls of river water. Mosquitoes also became a bother. "Hitherto, we had not suffered any inconveniences from mosquitoes," described Marquette, "but we were entering into their home, as it were." The pesky insects rose in swarms from swamps and river marshes. The explorers fought back by erecting crude tents of white sailcloth over their canoes. Beneath the canvas they escaped the mosquitoes as well as the burning rays of the sun.

Without knowing it, the Frenchmen drifted past the place where the exploring Spaniards had committed De Soto to a watery grave 131 years earlier. The sluggish Mississippi drew the expedition onward.

One day the Frenchmen noticed Indians armed with muskets lined along the shore. Though these natives seemed ready to attack, the Frenchmen bravely paddled toward them. Father Marquette held his Illinois calumet high in the air so the Indians could see the feath-

Marquette holding the Illinois calumet, which smoothed his introduction to Indian villages along the Mississippi

ered peace pipe. He called out to them in the Huron language, and the Indians shouted something back. ". . . they were as frightened as we were," Marquette quickly realized. The Indians eventually welcomed the French strangers ashore.

"We therefore landed," described Marquette, "and entered their Cabins, where they offered us meat from wild cattle [buffalo] and bear's grease, with white plums, which are very good." These Indians, possibly of the Chickasaw nation, possessed guns, hatchets, hoes, knives, cloth, and other items. They explained they obtained these trade goods from Europeans living to the east. It was clear these natives had contact with the Spanish colonists established along the coast of present-day Florida and Georgia. And these Indians told the French explorers something else. "They assured us," explained Marquette, "that we were no more than ten day's journey from The sea."

With rising excitement the explorers continued on their way. Just ten more days of paddling and they could reach their goal.

In the hot summer weather they coasted ahead. Cottonwood, elm, and basswood trees stood tall and thick along the riverbanks. From beyond these woods the explorers heard the bellowing of buffaloes as they grazed on prairie grass.

"We had gone down to near the 33rd degree of latitude," Marquette later wrote, "having proceeded nearly all the time in a southerly direction. . . ." The sound of yelling and war whoops suddenly broke the calm. The Frenchmen instantly noticed a large Indian village on the riverbank. Dozens of hostile natives ran back and forth beside the water's edge. "They were armed with bows, arrows, hatchets, clubs, and shields," exclaimed Marquette. Some screaming warriors shook their weapons at the frightened Frenchmen. Others pushed off shore aboard large canoes carved of solid wood. "They prepared to attack us, on both land and water," declared Marquette. A few young warriors flung themselves into the river. They tried to swim out to the French canoes. When the current proved too strong, they returned to shore. "One of them," exclaimed Marquette, "then hurled his club, which passed over without striking us."

Marquette holds the calumet aloft.

The fearful Frenchmen paddled fast, but escape seemed almost impossible. Indian canoes closed in from both upstream and downstream. Jolliet and the other traders prepared to defend themselves with their guns. All the while Father Marquette bravely held his calumet high so the Indians could see it. The dugout canoes edged close and forced the two birchbark canoes toward shore. Wild shouting filled the Frenchmen's ears. Warriors grabbed at the two canoes. Marquette still raised and lowered the calumet as a sign of peace.

". . . they were already prepared to pierce us with arrows from all sides," exclaimed the blackrobed priest, "when God suddenly touched the hearts of the old men, who were standing at the water's edge." Two of the village elders noticed the calumet and understood its peaceful meaning. Shouting loudly, they ordered the younger warriors to calm themselves. They demanded that the peace pipe be respected. The elders then threw their own bows and arrows aboard the French canoes and climbed aboard the boats themselves and made signs of apology. Many of the younger warriors still scowled as the Frenchmen were brought to shore. A few poked at the strange white canoes and laughed when their knives cut through the birchbark so easily. But the Frenchmen realized that at least their lives were safe. They glanced gratefully at the calumet still held by Father Marquette.

These Indians were members of the Quapaw nation. Their village, called Mitchigamea, lay on the west bank of the Mississippi several miles north of the mouth of the Arkansas River. Marquette and Jolliet tried speaking all of the Indian languages they knew. But these Quapaws understood none of them. An old man soon stepped forward who spoke a little Illinois. Jolliet passed out knives, hatchets, beads, and other presents from his stock of trade goods, while Marquette eagerly asked the old man questions. The other Frenchmen repaired the damaged canoes with birchbark patches, sticky rosin, and catgut thread. With sign language they explained to the curious Quapaws how the boats were made. That evening the Quapaw women provided the travelers with a feast of sagamite and roasted fish. At night the Frenchmen slept on shore. The old Indian interpreter had told Marquette that a larger Quapaw village called Akamsea lay about 30 miles (48 km) downstream. The natives there could better answer the Frenchmen's river questions.

"We embarked early on the following day," recorded Father Marquette. The old interpreter sat in one of the French canoes. Ten other Quapaws paddled a short distance ahead in one of their large dugout canoes. Word of the French had already reached Akamsea. A mile from the village a canoe of natives greeted the French voyagers. The chief of the village stood in the bow. In his hand he held a calumet.

The boats soon coasted to Akamsea. The Indian villagers lined the east riverbank as the Frenchmen stepped ashore. The chieftain sang a formal song of welcome and passed the tobacco pipe for smoking. He then led his guests through the village to his large cabin. It stood on a raised mound and was carpeted with woven reed mats. The Frenchmen sat in the place of honor. The chieftain and the village elders sat nearby. Dozens of Quapaw warriors crouched farther away, and dozens of common villagers squeezed into all corners of the great lodge.

Father Marquette carefully observed these Quapaws and how they lived. "The men go naked, and wear Their

Marquette and Jolliet with their Indian interpreter

hair short; they pierce their noses, from which, as well as from Their ears, hang beads. The women are clad in . . . [animal] skins; they knot Their hair in two tresses which they throw behind their ears. . . . Their Cabins, which are made of bark, are Long and Wide. . . . " Within the chieftain's lodge servants passed wooden platters of steaming sagamite, corn on the cob, and roasted dog meat. Marquette and Jolliet tried to talk with the Quapaws as they feasted. "Their language is exceedingly difficult," Marquette soon realized, "and I could succeed in pronouncing only a few words notwithstanding all my efforts." Luckily for the Europeans, a young man stepped forward who spoke Illinois much better than the old interpreter from Mitchigamea.

With the help of this boy, Marquette talked to the Quapaw leaders while Jolliet passed out presents. Marquette first preached about the Roman Catholic religion. It pleased the Jesuit priest that these Indians appeared interested in his words. "We afterward," he further noted, "asked them what they knew about the sea." The Quapaws nervously described the dangers that lay downstream. Fierce enemy Indians armed with guns fired at travelers who ventured to the south. Europeans lived at the mouth of the Mississippi, which was only days away. They traded hatchets, knives, and beads. The Quapaws obtained some of these valuable items from friendly Indians to the east and the west. But they rarely attempted to make visits downstream themselves.

In the darkness of evening the French explorers lay upon mats and drifted off to sleep. Suddenly a Quapaw awakened them and brought the bewildered men again before the chief. The chief had discovered village elders planning to kill and rob the Frenchmen. ". . . the Chief put a stop to all these plots," Marquette later wrote. "After sending for us, he danced the calumet before us . . . as a token of our entire safety; and to relieve us of all fear, he made me a present of it."

The explorers returned to bed, but now they tossed and turned. It would clearly not be wise to remain among the Quapaws too long. "Monsieur Jolliet and I held another Council," recalled Marquette, "to deliberate upon what we should do—whether we should push on, or remain content with the discovery which we had made." The expedition had fulfilled most of Intendant Talon's instructions. Marquette and Jolliet had found the Mississippi. They had explored 1,100 miles (1,770 km) of its course from the mouth of the Wisconsin River to the mouth of the Arkansas River. In spite of twists and turns, the giant waterway always carried them south. They were certain that the Mississippi did not lead west to the Orient.

The Frenchmen also realized that the Europeans at the Mississippi's mouth were likely rival Spaniards. "We further considered," Marquette later revealed, "that we exposed ourselves to the risk of losing the results of this voyage . . . if we proceeded to fling ourselves into the hands of the Spanish, who, without doubt, would at least have detained us as captives."

Their curiosity urged them onward, but caution halted them. The priest and the trader realized their grand journey must end here, or they might lose all they had gained. It was time to return home.

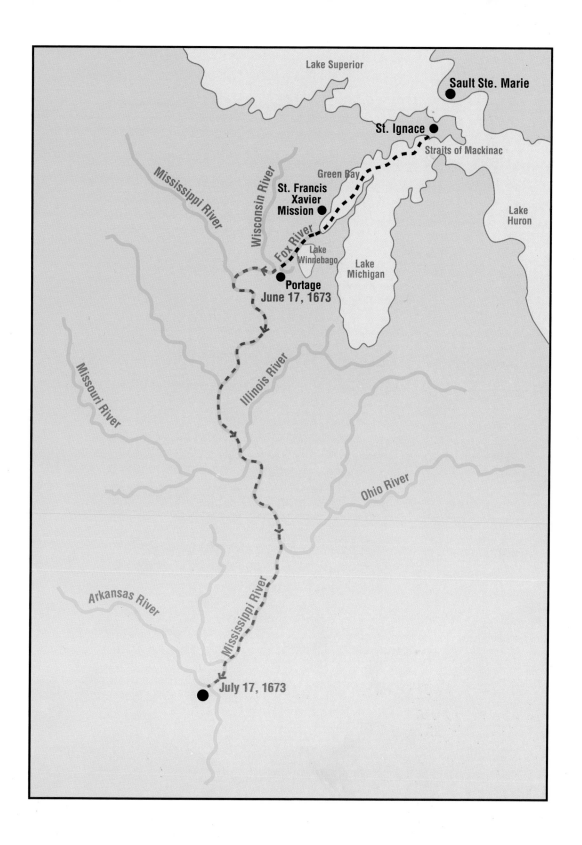

Chapter 8
Triumph and Disaster

The long journey upstream required strength and stamina. Traveling against the river current, every paddle stroke strained their muscles and energy. They stayed in the slack water close to shore whenever possible, but snags and sandbars often forced them into the deep water and a stronger current. The men squinted their eyes in the bright summer sunlight and paddled onward.

The work was tiring, but the voyagers traveled with confidence. They sometimes sang hymns or French folk songs while they paddled. In the evenings they gazed at the crackling flames of their riverside fires and thought of their friends and families awaiting their return in Canada. They knew the river now, and they smiled whenever they saw familiar landmarks. Friendly Indians waved as they passed the village of Mitchigamea. On August 4, they stopped again at the Chickasaw village and rested overnight.

The travelers return upriver.

Forging northward, the explorers toiled through the roaring currents at the mouth of the Ohio River and soon passed the wide mouth of the Missouri River. For a mile where the rivers merged, the raging water threatened to overturn the two canoes, but the Frenchmen pulled through the torrent with grunting strength. Above this place they stared again at the monsters painted on the rocky bluffs.

The voyagers reached the place where the Illinois River flowed into the Mississippi. The Peoria Indians had suggested the Illinois River as a short cut to Lake Michigan, and now Marquette and Jolliet decided to find out for themselves. Instead of continuing north on the Mississippi, the men paddled northeast along the banks of the Illinois. "We have seen nothing like this river that we enter as regards its fertility of soil, its prairies and woods," Father Marquette happily noted.

The Frenchmen hoisted their canvas sails. The canoes glided easily over the smooth water. Sitting comfortably, the voyagers enjoyed the scenery and wildlife they passed. Jolliet and his fur trading partners grinned when they spied beavers building wooden lodges beside the shore. They knew the beautiful Illinois River could provide trappers easy business opportunities.

After following the Illinois River for 200 miles (320 km) the explorers came upon a large Indian settlement. Father Marquette counted seventy-four cabins scattered along the riverside, each providing homes for two or three families. These Illinois Indians called this town Kaskaskia. It stood about 7 miles (11 km) downstream from the site of present-day Ottawa, Illinois. The Frenchmen went ashore and smoked the calumet with these friendly Indians. Village leaders described the countryside and answered the Frenchmen's questions. Jolliet's Indian boy played with children his own age. Adults and youngsters alike listened in awe as the voyagers described their amazing Mississippi journey. When Father Marquette preached to them, they weighed his words with quiet respect.

"They received us very well," Marquette remembered, "and obliged me to promise that I would return to instruct them." A chief of Kaskaskia offered to show the travelers the way to Lake Michigan. The Frenchmen gladly followed the Illinois chieftain and his escort of young warriors farther upstream. Where the clear waters of the Illinois forked into the Des Plaines River, the Indian guides led that way. The Indians showed the Frenchmen where they must carry their canoes a short distance overland, and at the end of the marshy trail, they reached the Chicago River. Swift strokes brought the group at last to the sandy shores and lapping waves of huge Lake Michigan.

The Frenchmen and the Illinois parted company here. Father Marquette silently vowed to return to Kaskaskia as soon as possible to perform missionary work among the Illinois.

The voyagers eagerly paddled up the western edge of Lake Michigan past beautiful trees and shrubs that reminded them of home. With happy smiles they understood that every paddle stroke now brought them closer to French civilization.

Before long the two canoes touched shore where a faint trail came down to the water. The men once again portaged their canoes through what is now Wisconsin's Door Peninsula to Sturgeon Bay. The men set the canoes down in the cold water with laughter and joking. The route before them was open and easy. Sturgeon Bay soon joined larger Green Bay. On the last day of their journey, the travelers coasted down Green Bay to the mouth of the Fox River. Yellow and orange autumn leaves fluttered onto the river surface as the excited explorers stroked the last short distance. On a day at the end of September 1673, they put ashore at the humble Jesuit mission of Saint Francis-Xavier. Four long months had passed since the explorers left this place. Their round-trip adventure had covered a distance of more than 2,900 miles (4,670 km).

As they stepped ashore, the seven Frenchmen surely knelt together beneath the trees and gave prayerful thanks for their safe return. The expedition had achieved its goal of finding and exploring the Mississippi. Father Marquette had found new peoples to whom the Roman Catholic faith could be preached. Louis Jolliet and his trading partners brought no furs back from the Mississippi wilderness, but the Missouri, Ohio, and Illinois Rivers all promised future profits.

No one greeted the explorers at Saint Francis-Xavier. The Menominee had gone into the deep woods for their autumn hunt. Father Allouez probably had traveled up the Fox to spend his winter among the Mascoutens. Sitting before the mission fireplace that night the explorers discussed their future plans. Jolliet and his trading partners were eager to return to Sault Sainte Marie. Marquette, however, decided to remain at Saint Francis-Xavier. Since leaving the lower Mississippi, the Jesuit priest had suffered bouts of sickness including feverish sweats, stomach cramps, and bloody diarrhea. Bad drinking water during the voyage could easily have given Marquette dysentery or typhoid fever. Therefore, he chose to rest and await the return of Father Allouez. The priest waved a weak good-bye as he watched his fellow explorers push off from the riverbank. Autumn breezes rippled the waters of Green Bay as the French traders paddled northward.

Shouts of joy greeted these travelers when they landed at Sault Sainte Marie. Zacharie Jolliet rushed to the waterside to hug his brother Louis and hear the story of the incredible journey down the Big River.

Cold October winds were blowing in Canada, so it was too late in the year to make the long journey to Quebec. Jolliet decided to spend the winter at Sault Sainte Marie.

The trading post kept Jolliet busy during the snowy days that winter. After work, at night, he prepared his

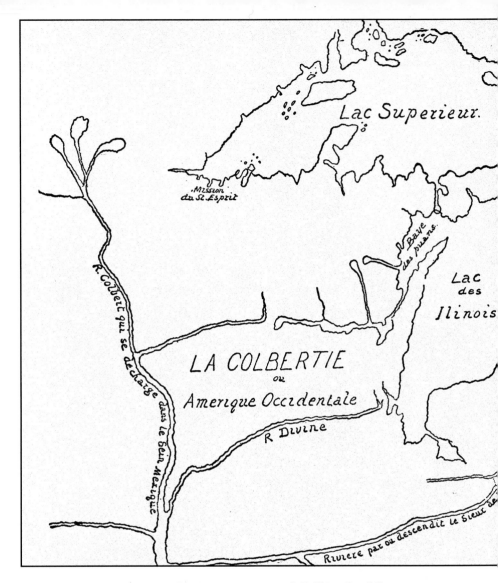

Mississippi report. Both Marquette and Jolliet had kept journals describing their river explorations. Jolliet also had drawn a map showing their discoveries. By the flickering light of cozy cabin fires, he wrote a revised copy of his journal. Dipping his quill pen in ink, he sketched a copy of his map as well. He left these valuable documents in the care of the Jesuits at the mission of Sault Sainte Marie.

Spring of 1674 arrived, and when the ice on St. Marys River broke up, Louis and Zacharie packed bundles of beaver pelts aboard one of Jolliet's canoes.

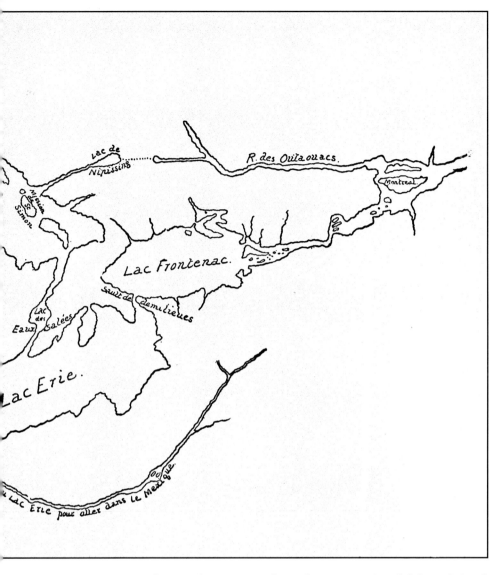

One of Jolliet's maps (redrawn years later).

Louis also took a strongbox that contained his original Mississippi journal and map. He carefully tucked away his compass, astrolabe, and Indian souvenirs from his trip. Zacharie would remain at the trading post, while Louis paddled to Quebec to report to the governor, the Count de Frontenac. (Two other Frenchmen also took places in the canoe, but their names are unknown.) Another place was saved for the Indian boy. Jolliet had grown very fond of the Illinois boy and treated him almost like a son. After months of living with the Jolliets, the boy now spoke French fairly well.

Jolliet and his companions paddled down the St. Marys River and along the northern shore of Lake Huron. By the end of June the travelers had reached the St. Lawrence River and were just upstream from Montreal. One difficult stretch, the Lachine Rapids, stood in their way. Jolliet's keen desire to reach the town clouded his judgment. Instead of submitting to the slow, arduous work of portaging, he chose to ride through the rapids.

The men gripped their paddles and steered forward. The river flowed fast, over and around the rocks. The canoe shot ahead. White water splashed into the boat, soaking the travelers. They shouted with excitement as they guided the canoe through each set of rocks. Before long the canoe had passed through forty-one of the rapids. Only one more stretch of rock-filled water remained. The men paddled hard, turning left and right to avoid sudden dangers. Then, in a terrible instant, they lost control. The surging current tossed the canoe against a rock. The fragile birchbark tore open, and the wooden slats cracked. The three Frenchmen, the Indian boy, the strongbox, and the beaver pelts were all flung into the wild river. Jolliet flailed his arms, but the raging water dragged him under.

By chance, two Frenchmen fishing below the rapids noticed a body tossed on the foaming water. Hurrying closer along the shore, they found the soaked, limp body lying against a low boulder. They pulled the unconscious man from the water and worked to bring him back to life. The man's lungs soon emptied, and water poured from his blue lips. Louis Jolliet spit and coughed and sucked in air. He opened his eyes and tried to sit up. Soon enough he realized his tragedy. The joy and success of his months of exploration had been destroyed

Count de Frontenac

in a horrible moment. He shuddered and wept. Only he had survived the crash. The others had drowned.

Jolliet regained his strength at Montreal. He traveled onward to Quebec, where he wrote his grim report for the Count de Frontenac: "It is not long since I am back from my voyage to the Sea of the South. I was favored by good fortune during the whole time, but on my return, when I was about to reach Montreal, my canoe capsized and I lost two men and a box wherein were all my papers, my journal, as well as some curios from those far off countries. I am much grieved over the loss of a ten-year-old boy who had been presented to me. He was of good disposition, quick-witted . . . and obedient." In broken spirits Jolliet woefully concluded, ". . . all I saved is my life."

Chapter 9
Glory for a Jesuit Priest

Freezing winds howled outside the mission of St. Francis-Xavier. Through the winter months of 1673-1674 Jacques Marquette remained inside the log cabin. He seemed to recover from his illness and soon felt well enough to preach to those Indians who came to camp beside the mission. At night he found time to fulfill another duty. He spread his Mississippi notes upon the wooden mission table. Upon sheets of clean paper, he carefully penned a finished copy of his journal. After completing that task he placed a larger blank sheet of paper on the table. Though he lacked Jolliet's professional skill, the Jesuit priest drew a crude map of the Mississippi and the rivers that joined it, as well as he understood them.

The importance of these documents became evident soon enough. In the spring of 1674, bad news arrived from Sault Sainte Marie. During a riot between visiting rival Sioux and Cree Indians, the mission house caught fire. Scorching flames poured from the windows. Burning timbers crashed to the ground. The mission and all its contents were destroyed, including the copy of Jolliet's journal. As a result of Jolliet's double misfortune, Marquette's journal became the only lasting detailed record of the Mississippi voyage.

As the weather warmed, Father Marquette's greatest wish was to return to the Illinois Indians of Kaskaskia. His lifelong dream of Roman Catholic missionary work among a new native nation finally seemed within his grasp. But disease still lurked within his tall, thin body. During the spring and summer months, burning fever and dysentery kept Marquette sick in bed. Having returned to the mission, Father Claude Allouez and Father Gabriel Druillettes nursed their brother priest as best as they could. Marquette sipped at herb tea and endured bleedings, a treatment believed to draw out the poisons in his body.

Marquette falls ill.

When Marquette eventually regained his strength in the fall, Henri Nouvel, Father Superior of the Jesuit mission at St. Ignace, granted Marquette the permission to return to Kaskaskia. Trappers Jacques Largillier and Pierre Porteret, who had shared in the original journey, now volunteered to return down the Mississippi with Marquette. The men packed their provisions, to which Father Marquette added his Mass Kit and other items he would need to spread his religion among the Indians. The three men pushed off from St. Francis-Xavier on October 25, 1674.

Raw winds and choppy waters greeted the men at the mouth of the Fox River as they entered Green Bay. They paddled up the east shore and on October 26 met five canoes of Potawatomie and four of Illinois at Sturgeon Bay. This trading party of fifty Indians was also traveling to the Illinois country. For safety, the Frenchmen and the Indians agreed to journey together.

The combined fleet of canoes made slow progress. Crossing the boggy ground from Sturgeon Bay to Lake Michigan required two full days, and it took many more days to travel south along the lake shore. At night around the campfires Father Marquette often preached to the Indians.

Winter had overtaken the weary group by November 23. "Then the cold began," recalled Marquette, "and more than a foot of snow covered the ground." During this three-day blizzard Pierre Porteret shot a deer, three ducks, and three turkeys, which kept the stew pot filled. Marquette, however, had very little appetite. The cold weather and long delays had caused a return of his ill health. They traveled slowly as Father Marquette burned with fever and suffered painful attacks of dysentery.

Site of Chicago, Illinois (Chicago River is in the foreground, leading to Lake Michigan)

Lake Michigan began to freeze under the December cold. The paddlers carefully steered the canoes between floating patches of ice. On December 4, they reached the mouth of the Chicago River (where downtown Chicago, Illinois, today stands). Great drifts of snow covered the riverbanks, and the river itself was frozen over with ice a foot thick. The travelers dragged their canoes ashore. They staggered through the snow and threw together crude shelters of branches covered with buffalo skins and canvas. Jacques Largillier and Pierre Porteret soon realized that Father Marquette was too ill to travel in such frigid weather. To escape the fierce winds blowing off Lake Michigan, on December 12 the travelers pulled their canoes and baggage a few miles farther into the woods.

"Having encamped," explained Marquette, ". . . two leagues up the river, we resolved to winter there, as it was impossible to go farther . . . and my ailment did not permit me to give myself much [rest]." The men built a rough hut and settled inside. Stalking wild game Largillier and Porteret shot down three buffalo and four deer in the forest. The Frenchmen's Indian friends traded warm buffalo robes for meat and tobacco before they continued to Kaskaskia. "Chachagwessiou and the other Illinois left us," revealed Marquette's journal entry for December 15, "to go and join their people."

During the last days of December, Jacques Largillier hiked nearly 20 miles (32 km) to the closest Illinois village. He returned with news on December 30. Pierre Moreau, who had been one of the seven Mississippi explorers, was trading in the area with a French partner called "The Surgeon." When he learned that Marquette was ill, The Surgeon tramped over 50 miles (80 km) of snowy terrain to give the ill priest a gift of blueberries and corn. Indian traders also helped keep the stranded Frenchmen supplied with food. "3 Illinois brought us . . . 2 sacks of corn, some dried meat [and] pumpkins," wrote Marquette on January 26.

Each day Largillier and Porteret watched over the Jesuit priest. By February 9 Marquette reported, ". . . all that remains is a weakness of the stomach. I am beginning to feel much better, and to regain my strength." From the snugness of their riverside shelter, the three Frenchmen watched for signs of spring. On March 28 the river ice began breaking up. Ice chunks flowed downstream on the suddenly moving river torrent. Through the next hours the water level rose so fast it threatened to flood the Frenchmen's camp. The three men hastily hung their gear in high tree branches. That night they slept uncomfortably on a nearby hilltop. "The water gained on us nearly all night," exclaimed Marquette afterwards, "but there was a slight freeze, and the water fell a little. . . ." The Frenchmen took this opportunity to load their canoe, and on March 30 they embarked once again.

The men paddled hard while battling bitterly cold winds and rough water. Near the headwaters of the Chicago River, the Frenchmen crossed overland in bitter weather to the banks of the Des Plaines River. Paddling on its swirling current, the three voyagers rode downstream and entered the Illinois River. On April 10, 1675, Marquette and his two assistants finally coasted ashore at Kaskaskia. The village had grown since Marquette had seen it last. More than 3,000 men, women, and children crowded to the riverbank with smiles and happy greetings for the blackrobe. These Illinois had gathered at Kaskaskia to hear the holy words Marquette had promised them. Everywhere the blackrobe walked the Indians crowded close around him. Marquette chose a wide prairie beside the village as the best place for his open-air church.

On Thursday April 11, the Illinois covered the ground with woven mats and soft bearskins. At the front sat the chiefs and village elders. Warriors, women, and children pressed in a large semi-circle behind them. At the front of this assembly, Largillier and Porteret hammered two poles into the ground and strung a line between them. They unrolled pieces of rich red Chinese taffeta cloth and draped them over the line. On this cloth they hung the four large pictures of the Virgin Mary that Father Marquette had brought on the journey. The Indians gazed in wonder at the colorful portraits that hung before them.

When all was ready, Father Marquette stepped before the assembly and began his preaching. Ten times he presented the Illinois chiefs with gifts to symbolize the importance of his messages.

During the next three days, which were Good Friday, Holy Saturday, and Easter Sunday, he continued preaching at Kaskaskia. At the end of each day, the tall, pale priest celebrated Mass. Sometimes he felt faint or clutched his stomach because his illness had returned. With religious fervor, though, he kept at his work among the Illinois.

After Easter Sunday, Largillier and Porteret gently packed away the pictures and Chinese taffeta. At the waterside they loaded the baggage aboard their worn old canoe. Already it was time for Father Marquette to start northward. He was expected to report at St. Ignace at Michilimackinac that spring. All of the villagers of Kaskaskia followed the respected blackrobe to the riverbank. They offered him gifts and asked that he return to them as soon as possible. Seated at the center of the canoe, he waved a cheerful farewell as Largillier and Porteret started paddling.

Dozens of Illinois honored the Jesuit priest by escorting the Frenchmen upriver. Each night during the eleven-day trip they camped together. Father Marquette remained smiling and full of warm affection for his Indian companions, but Largillier and Porteret noticed the dimming of his eyes and the weakness of his voice.

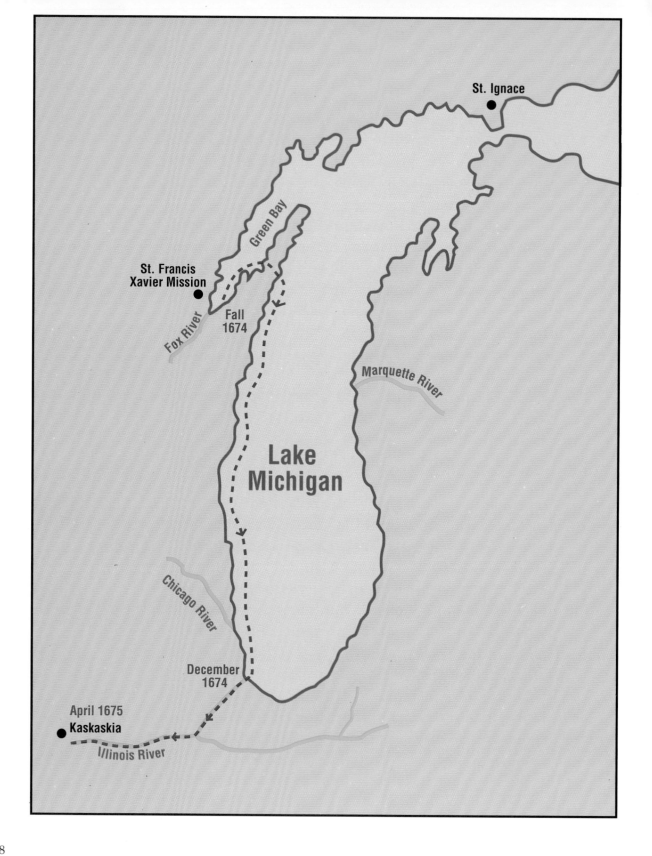

St. Ignace

St. Francis
Xavier Mission

Green Bay

Fox River

Fall
1674

Marquette River

**Lake
Michigan**

Chicago River

December
1674

April 1675
Kaskaskia

Illinois River

Upon reaching Lake Michigan, the Frenchmen and the Illinois parted company. By this time Father Marquette was clearly ill. "Indeed, he became so feeble and exhausted," Father Dablon later learned, "that he was unable to assist or even to move himself, and had to be handled and carried about like a child." This time, Largillier and Porteret steered the canoe up the eastern coast of Lake Michigan. They hoped this unexplored route would save them time in reaching the mission of St. Ignace. Bending over their paddles with quick rhythm, the two faithful servants began the last stretch of 300 miles (480 km).

Father Marquette hardly noticed the lush, wooded meadows along the shore. He lay in the canoe crippled with fever and pain. Still, he never complained. At night beside their lonely campfires, Largillier and Porteret spooned warm broth into the sick man's mouth. They bathed his face and arms with cool lake water. They prayed for him, but they saw that he was sinking fast.

Each day they pushed father north. The travelers passed the mouths of the St. Joseph, the Black, and the Kalamazoo rivers. At times while they paddled, Largillier and Porteret heard Marquette praying softly. They sadly realized they would never reach St. Ignace in time. Marquette understood his fate and gladly accepted it. It would be his final sacrifice to Jesuit missionary service. "The evening before his death . . ." recorded Father Dablon, "he told them very Joyously, that it would take place on the morrow. He conversed with them during the whole Day as to what would need to be done for his burial. . . ."

The next day, on May 17, 1675, Marquette chose a place along the shore and weakly asked that the canoe stop there. Largillier and Porteret lifted him ashore and

The death of Marquette

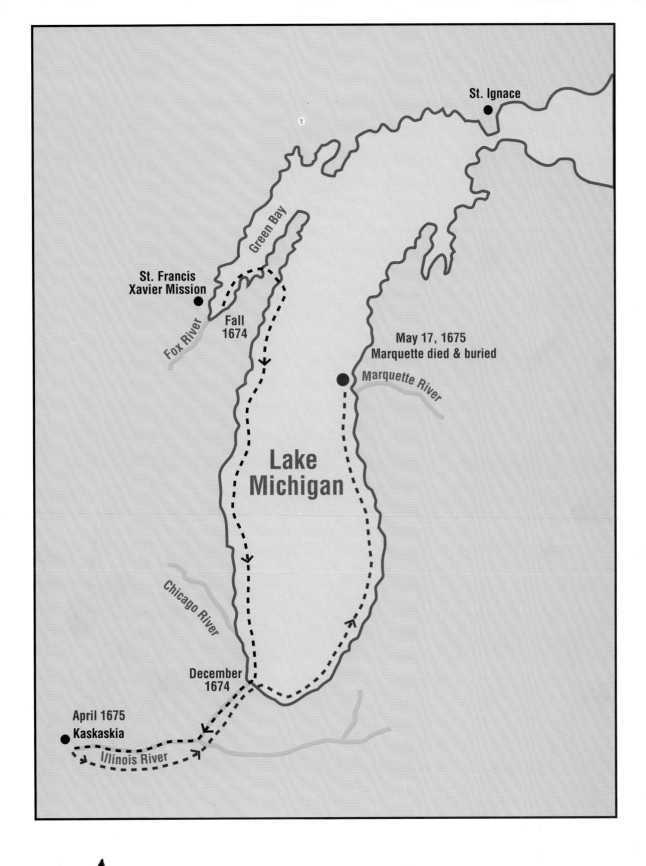

St. Ignace

St. Francis
Xavier Mission

Green Bay

Fox River

Fall
1674

May 17, 1675
Marquette died & buried

Marquette River

Lake
Michigan

Chicago River

December
1674

April 1675
Kaskaskia

Illinois River

carried him to the heights of a bluff that overlooked the water. They lay the priest on the ground and quickly built a shelter. In this wild but peaceful place, Marquette softly uttered a few final words of faith. Then he closed his eyes forever. At the age of nearly thirty-eight years, Father Jacques Marquette died. His weeping comrades buried him on the hillside near the place where the Pere Marquette River flows into Lake Michigan near present-day Ludington, Michigan.

Jacques Largillier and Pierre Porteret paddled home. They reached Michilimackinac at the end of May, and they reported their sad news to the Jesuit priests at St. Ignace. In the spring of 1677, a band of Ottawa Indians were hunting and trading along Lake Michigan. Father Marquette had preached to these people five years earlier. Full of love for their dead teacher they stopped at Marquette's gravesite. Following solemn Indian custom they dug up the grave and respectfully brought the Jesuit priest's bones back to the mission of St. Ignace. Father Henri Nouvel laid the bones to final rest in a vault beneath the mission floor. Canadian Frenchman and Indians alike mourned the loss of the dedicated priest. ". . . the range of his zeal . . . made him carry the Faith to the ends of this new world," praised Father Claude Dablon. At the time of his death, no Frenchman had traveled farther throughout North America. Father Jacques Marquette had fulfilled his destiny.

Present-day gravesite of Marquette at St. Ignace, Michigan

Chapter 10
Profit and Loss

". . . after having passed through a thousand dangers, he had . . . unfortunately been wrecked . . . his Canoe having upset . . . near Montreal, where he lost both his men and his papers, and whence he escaped only by a sort of Miracle."

With these words Father Claude Dablon described Louis Jolliet's return to Quebec in the summer of 1674. On the heels of his Ottawa River disaster came the news of the fire at Sault Sainte Marie. Jolliet wrote another journal and drew another map from memory, but these sketches lacked the first-hand details of his original documents.

Jolliet returned to the life of a Quebec trader and merchant. Even before he left on his Mississippi voyage, a young Quebec woman named Claire-Francoise Bissot had attracted his attention. Now he courted her in earnest, escorting her to dances and church services. The explorer soon won her heart completely. Family and friends filled the pews of the Cathedral of Quebec on October 7, 1675. Thirty-year-old Louis Jolliet must have felt unusual dressed in a handsome suit of clothes instead of rough buckskins. Nineteen-year-old Claire-Francoise Bissot smiled sweetly as she walked the aisle in a white muslin gown ornamented with fine lace. They exchanged wedding vows and began their lives as husband and wife.

The Jolliets settled into a house in the lower town of Quebec. During their happy marriage they eventually would have six children. With a growing family, Jolliet worked harder than ever to make his trading business a success.

The news of Father Marquette's death saddened Jolliet. Their time together exploring the Mississippi remained vivid in his mind. In 1676, Jolliet asked the French government to recognize his trading rights in the region of the Illinois. He wished to establish a trading post on the Illinois River. An official answer arrived from France in the spring of 1677. The government turned down his request, explaining: "The number of [French] settlers in Canada should be increased before thinking of settlements elsewhere. . . ."

Deeply disappointed, Jolliet continued his Canadian business activities. Zacharie Jolliet sent bundles of rich beaver pelts from the trading post at Sault Sainte Marie. Louis sold these pelts, as well as crates of dried codfish and barrels of seal-oil, from his Quebec warehouse.

Jolliet took on a new partner, Jacques de Lalande, a relative of his wife. In 1679 the French government granted Jolliet and Lalande exclusive trading rights at all of the islands and waterways at Mingan. Located near the mouth of the St. Lawrence River (downstream from Quebec), Mingan promised to be a valuable site for fishing cod and hunting seal. It seemed that the French government had decided to give Jolliet a reward for his exploration of the Mississippi after all.

As a trader, Jolliet took keen interest in Canadian political developments. Both France and England made claims on the vast region surrounding Hudson Bay to the north, though it was unexplored. With each passing season, fewer Indians brought their furs to French trading posts. Rumors reached Quebec that scheming English traders were establishing rival posts on Hudson Bay. In the spring of 1679, the new intendant, Jacques Duchesneau, sent for Jolliet. He asked that the skilled explorer journey to Hudson Bay and investigate the situation. The thought of renewed adventures thrilled Jolliet, and he accepted without hesitation.

Jolliet rounded up a traveling party of seven men, including himself and his brother Zacharie. On May 13, 1679, they set forth in three canoes, coasting down the St. Lawrence River. Before long Jolliet and his men reached the rocky place where the Saguenay River flows into the St. Lawrence. Jolliet chose to follow the Saguenay toward Hudson Bay. Through the difficult days ahead the voyagers paddled past rocky shores and forests of spruce trees. As they passed farther northward the woods grew sparse and scraggly. The land became tundra covered only by moss and short grasses. Ducks, geese, and other migratory birds nested beside marshy pools.

No direct water route connected the St. Lawrence River and Hudson Bay, so the adventurers were forced to portage more than 125 times. The Rupert River at last led the travelers to salt water. On a bright, windy day they suddenly found James Bay spreading ahead of them. James Bay formed the most southerly part of huge Hudson Bay.

Jolliet immediately found the English. Near the mouth of the Rupert River stood a fort of rough timbers. A ship with twelve cannon floated quietly at anchor. Jolliet fired a pistol into the air. The noise brought four surprised English hunters out of the nearby woods. These men escorted Jolliet and his comrades into the fort. The redcoat soldiers inside stared at their French visitors with suspicion. Before long, however, Charles Bayly, the English governor of Hudson Bay, arrived to greet his unexpected guests.

"You are welcome, sir," he told Jolliet; "you came here with peaceful intentions and you have nothing to fear." Bayly knew of Jolliet and his discovery of the Mississippi. With friendly admiration he invited the Frenchman to dinner. In a private room, the two men sipped glasses of sparkling wine. Bayly spoke of life on Hudson Bay and Jolliet listened carefully. The governor boasted that in addition to Fort Rupert there were three other English forts in the region to support the growing English fur trade. It seemed clear the English intended to stay. Bayly even offered to hire Jolliet to work for him. As a loyal Frenchmen, Jolliet politely turned down this bold proposal. Instead he and his men started for home the next day.

On October 5, 1679, the seven explorers returned, and Jolliet promptly reported to the intendant. If the French wished to compete for the northern fur trade, he concluded, they must venture into the region as soon as possible. Several Quebec merchants followed this advice and formed a new trading company.

His summer of exploration was over, and Jolliet returned to his own business interests in Quebec and at Mingan. In 1680, the French government rewarded Jolliet more fully for his loyal service. Near Mingan at the mouth of the St. Lawrence River stood Anticosti Island. This valuable piece of land stretched more than 75 miles (120 km) from east to west and covered 2,500,000 acres (1,012,000 hectares). ". . . in consideration of his discovery of the Illinois country . . . and of the voyage which he has just made to Hudson Bay

Anticosti Island in winter

in behalf of and to the advantage of the . . . colony," proclaimed the official document, Jolliet was presented with the prize of Anticosti Island.

Jolliet built a cabin on the western coast of Anticosti Island. The rocky island controlled the best seal and cod fisheries of the entire St. Lawrence region. Throwing out his fishing nets that summer of 1680, Jolliet felt like a lucky man indeed. Through the next ten years, he prospered at Anticosti. He shipped boatloads of dried codfish to Quebec every fall. Ships sailing up and down the St. Lawrence often stopped to trade with the well-known Frenchman. Servants kept black cauldrons heated to render seal blubber into valuable lighting oil. Jolliet's children grew up exploring the woods and meadows of the wild island in the brave tradition of their father.

French-Canadian relations with the Iroquois Indians of New York and the English colonists of New England remained tense. In 1690, warfare broke out as the struggle for trading rights and land flared up. On a bright October day, while Louis and the three oldest Jolliet boys were fishing miles away, Claire-Francoise Jolliet noticed white sails on the horizon. Thirty-two English ships were approaching from the Gulf of St. Lawrence. Sir William Phips of Boston commanded this enemy fleet with the intention of attacking Quebec. On the way, he decided to raid Anticosti Island.

With frightened shouts Claire-Francoise alerted the Jolliet settlement. Family and servants alike hoisted sail and tried to escape by boat up the St. Lawrence River. The Jolliets escaped, but the English sailors ransacked the Anticosti warehouse. They carried off valuable beaver, otter, and fox pelts, as well as the boxes of knives, pots, mirrors, and other trade goods Jolliet stored there. Rampaging soldiers tore through Jolliet's house, smashing china and ripping bedspreads. They finally burned the entire settlement to the ground.

Sailing onward, the English fleet overtook Claire-Francoise Jolliet's little boat. The Jolliets were taken prisoner, and the English fleet moved on. As prisoners aboard Phips's flagship, the Jolliet family witnessed the English attack on Quebec on October 16. Thundering ships' cannon sent cannonballs crashing into the streets of the city. From the high plateau above the river, French cannoneers answered with guns of their own. One blast shattered a mast on the English flagship. Phips ordered his fleet out of range, but first set the Jolliets free in a prisoner exchange. Upon his return to Quebec, Louis Jolliet learned that his wife and children were safe. For that he gave prayers of thanks.

The attack on Quebec

Charred ruins and smoky ashes greeted Jolliet's return to Anticosti Island. He tried rebuilding his settlement, but in 1691 English ships again sailed up the Gulf of St. Lawrence just far enough to raid Anticosti Island. The looting and burning of his new settlement put Jolliet out of business and into debt.

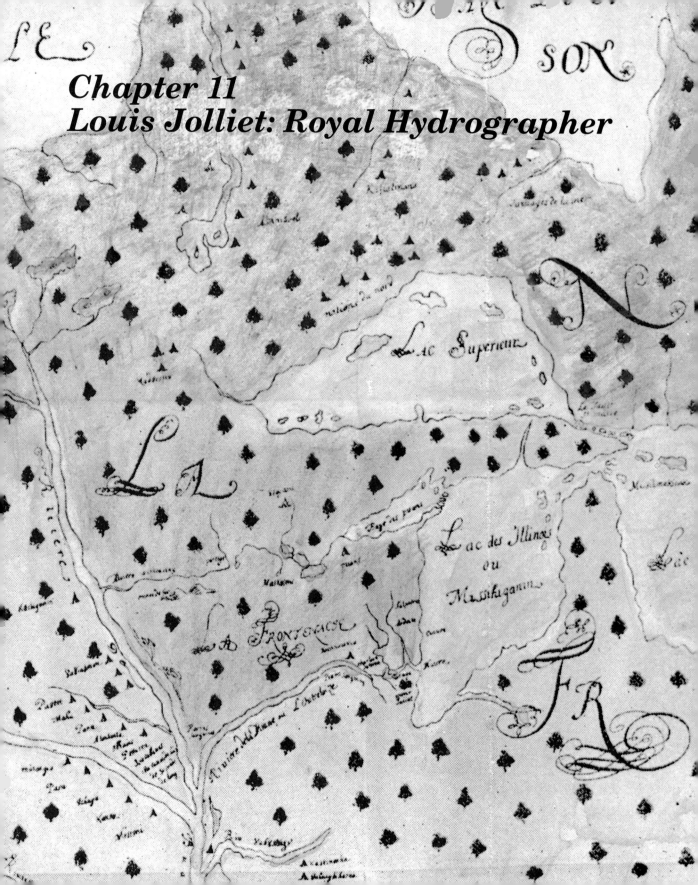

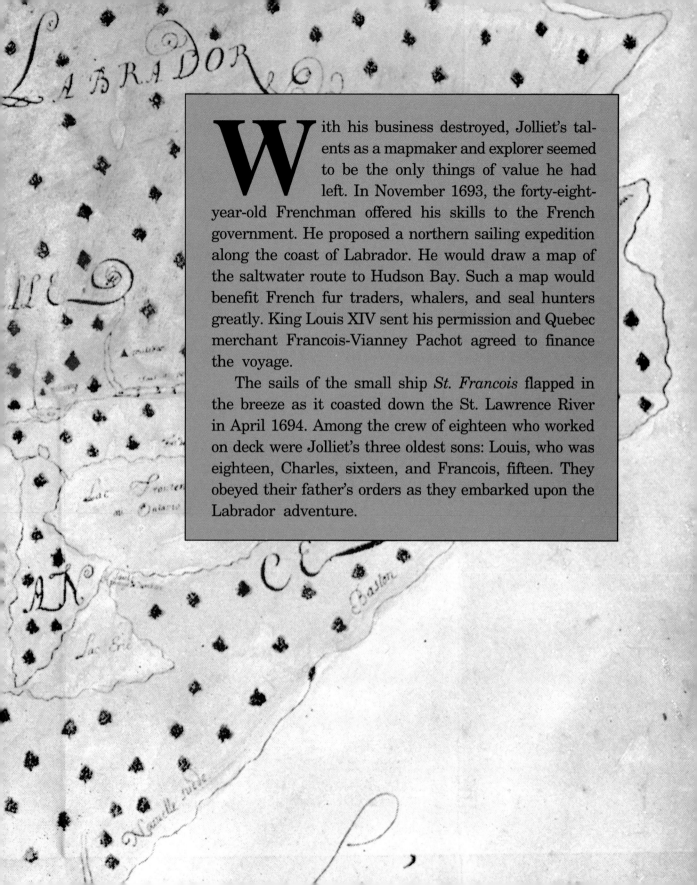

With his business destroyed, Jolliet's talents as a mapmaker and explorer seemed to be the only things of value he had left. In November 1693, the forty-eight-year-old Frenchman offered his skills to the French government. He proposed a northern sailing expedition along the coast of Labrador. He would draw a map of the saltwater route to Hudson Bay. Such a map would benefit French fur traders, whalers, and seal hunters greatly. King Louis XIV sent his permission and Quebec merchant Francois-Vianney Pachot agreed to finance the voyage.

The sails of the small ship *St. Francois* flapped in the breeze as it coasted down the St. Lawrence River in April 1694. Among the crew of eighteen who worked on deck were Jolliet's three oldest sons: Louis, who was eighteen, Charles, sixteen, and Francois, fifteen. They obeyed their father's orders as they embarked upon the Labrador adventure.

The great northeastern Canadian region called Labrador remained a great mystery to Europeans. Jolliet knew the Labrador coast along the St. Lawrence River and Gulf of St. Lawrence perhaps better than any man. He had fished beside its rocky shores and river inlets for years. Through the wet, foggy days of May and June the *St. Francois* slowly sailed ahead. The sailors heard the noise of gulls whirling overhead and the splashing of the waves against the shoreline rocks. Jolliet slowly traced a coastal map, every day adding the outlines of new coves, islands, and other landmarks.

The ship eventually entered the Strait of Belle Isle, which separated Labrador from the huge island of Newfoundland. Passing through the narrow waterway the voyagers reached the open green waters of the Atlantic Ocean on July 11. The *St. Francois* hugged the Labrador coast as it edged northward. In the distance the French sailors saw blue-white icebergs floating slowly like giant mountains on the ocean current. One morning noises like deafening cannon shots startled the explorers. An iceberg was breaking up, and each massive piece splashed into the water creating giant waves.

Rowing ashore one day Jolliet shot a caribou. That night the happy sailors ate meat instead of their boring diet of fish. Jolliet proudly hung the animal's antlers on the ship's mast. On July 15, the Frenchmen saw two sealskin boats gliding out from shore. The two Native American Eskimos who paddled these kayaks shouted "Tcharacou! Tcharacou!" which Jolliet believed meant "Peace! Peace!" The two smiling natives signaled their desire. "They invited us to come and anchor in a nearby cove," explained Jolliet. "We could do our trading there, they said. . . ." The French landed only long enough to swap a few knives for a few sealskins.

The rough seas on the Labrador Coast

Jolliet steered the *St. Francois* farther along the Labrador coast. Even in the summer sunshine, chilly winds reminded the voyagers how far north they already had traveled. On July 22, six more native kayaks appeared on the water. The Eskimos sitting in them waved for the Frenchmen to come ashore. Jolliet and several of his crewmen rowed a ship's boat to land. A dozen sealskin lodges stood on the moss-covered rocks. Village natives traded sealskins and perhaps some carved whale bones for the knives and other valued items Jolliet offered. The *St. Francois* remained anchored at this place for five days. On one occasion a group of native women entertained the visitors. They sang songs in lovely voices while rhythmically stamping their booted feet. The French responded by chanting a hymn and singing cheerful French-Canadian folk songs.

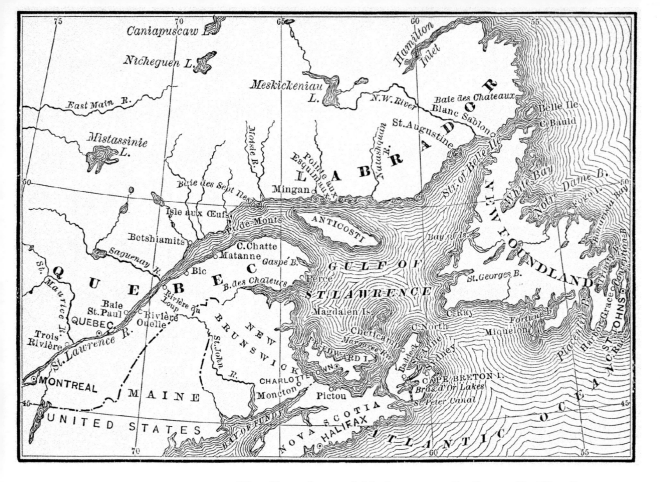

The Frenchmen bid these people farewell. The flapping sails of the *St. Francois* carried the voyagers farther northward. Along the way other curious natives greeted them and traded the few sealskins they possessed. The first days of August found Jolliet faithfully charting every bay and curve of the coastline on his map. When the ship neared present-day Nunasaluk Island at about 57 degrees north latitude, the voyagers reached a decision. "Seeing then. . . ." Jolliet penned in his sea journal, "since summer was already far advanced and we were in a country where it is always cold, where icebergs are found the whole year round, and where the hills, valleys and the tops of the mountains are always covered with snow . . . we unanimously resolved to find a harbor where we could condition the ship for the return journey to Quebec."

While anchored, the sailors repaired worn ropes and patched torn canvas sails. On August 16, 1694, the *St. Francois* started southward on its return journey. Slipping through the Strait of Belle Isle, the Frenchmen paused in the Gulf of St. Lawrence to fill their fishing nets with cod. With this profitable cargo, the *St. Francois* anchored in Quebec harbor in the middle of October.

Jolliet's chart of the Labrador coast increased his fine reputation as a mapmaker. In 1695, the Count de Frontenac hired the skilled navigator to draw up official charts of the St. Lawrence River. In November of that year, the captain of the ship *Charente* demanded that an expert pilot guide his ship from Quebec out to sea. No one knew the course better than Jolliet, so he said good-bye to his wife and children and began a new journey.

The voyage of the *Charente* carried Jolliet across the stormy Atlantic all the way to France. The Count de Frontenac had entrusted Jolliet with letters for the French government. Jolliet also carried copies of his maps he hoped to show. From the port of La Rochelle, he traveled the snow-covered French countryside to the court of Louis XIV. Perhaps it was at the grand royal palace at Versailles that the humble wheelwright's son was ushered into the presence of the French king. Jolliet delivered his letters and unrolled his maps. Frontenac's letters praised Jolliet's services to the crown, and the king and his advisors recognized Jolliet's obvious talents as a mapmaker. When Jolliet sailed for home in the spring of 1696, he carried with him a document stamped with the royal seal. It named him Royal Hydrographer, the King's Map Maker of Quebec. At the same time he had been appointed to teach the art of chartmaking at the Jesuit College in Quebec.

Statue of Louis Jolliet

These honors kept Jolliet busy in Quebec in the upcoming winters. During the days he taught his Jesuit pupils at the college. At night by flickering candlelight, Jolliet carefully sketched his maps with colored inks. As the colony's Royal Hydrographer he completed a fine map of the St. Lawrence River.

Fishing and trading at Mingan and at Anticosti Island occupied the gray-haired Jolliet during his summers. The sights and sounds of that sunny season always warmed his heart.

It is unknown exactly how Louis Jolliet died, but at the end of the summer of 1700, the fifty-five-year-old mapmaker was buried at Mingan. On September 15, 1700, bells at Quebec's Cathedral of Notre Dame tolled mournfully. The Jesuit priests there held a memorial service for the man who had played the church organ so many Sundays.

With the passage of time, the names Marquette and Jolliet became forever linked together. Wherever the waters of the Mississippi flow, there flow the spirits of Jacques Marquette and Louis Jolliet. Their exploration of the upper Mississippi marked their greatest fame. After them, the Sieur de La Salle paddled all the way to the mouth of the Mississippi in 1682. For the next eighty years, the French held the greatest European claim to the vast western river lands they called the Louisiana Territory. In 1803, President Thomas Jefferson paid fifteen million dollars to purchase Louisiana, and the Mississippi River became the heart of the United States.

Marquette and Jolliet

Timeline of Events in Marquette's and Jolliet's Lifetime

1637 — Jacques Marquette is born on June 1 in Laon, France

1643 — Future explorer Rene-Robert Cavelier, Sieur de La Salle is born in Rouen, France

1645 — Louis Jolliet is born near Quebec City, New France

1646 — Jacques Marquette enrolls in the Jesuit college at Reims

1656 — Marquette begins his studies to join the Jesuit order

1661 — French king Louis XIV begins his reign

1662 — Louis Jolliet begins studying for the Jesuit priesthood

1666 — Marquette is ordained a Jesuit priest and goes to New France as a missionary

1667 — Jolliet is released from his Jesuit studies

1668 — Marquette establishes a mission among the Ottawa Indians at Sault Sainte Marie; Jolliet becomes a fur trader

1669 — Marquette goes to the St. Esprit mission on Lake Superior to work among the Huron and Ottawa Indians; Jolliet begins exploring the Great Lakes region for the New France government; his brother Adrien dies, and Louis Jolliet carries on his fur-trading business; La Salle begins an exploration up the St. Lawrence River

1670 — Jolliet sets up a fur-trading post at Sault Sainte Marie

1671 — Marquette moves to the St. Ignace mission on northern Lake Michigan

1672 — Count de Frontenac, governor of New France, appoints Louis Jolliet to find and explore the Mississippi River; Jolliet asks Marquette to go with him

1673 — Marquette and Jolliet set out from St. Ignace mission at Michilimackinac, following the Fox and Wisconsin rivers to the Mississippi; they travel as far as the mouth of the Arkansas River, then return up the Mississippi to New France

1674 — In a canoe accident on the way to Montreal, Jolliet loses the original copy of his Mississippi expedition journal and almost drowns; the only extra copy of Jolliet's journal of the Mississippi River expedition is destroyed in a fire at Sault Sainte Marie; Marquette travels from St. Francis-Xavier mission (near present-day Green Bay, Wisconsin) to preach to the Kaskaskia Indians (in present-day Illinois)

1675 — Marquette arrives at Kaskaskia and preaches to the Indians, although he is ill; on his return trip to St. Ignace, he dies near present-day Ludington, Michigan, on May 17; Jolliet marries Claire-Francoise Bissot in Quebec

1678 — La Salle begins exploring the Mississippi River Valley

1679 — Jolliet is sent to Canada's Hudson Bay to investigate English fur-trading operations

1680 — The French government rewards Jolliet for his services by giving him Anticosti Island at the mouth of the St. Lawrence River

1682 — La Salle reaches the mouth of the Mississippi River at the Gulf of Mexico

1687 — La Salle is murdered by members of his expedition

1689 — Jolliet explores the coast of present-day Labrador

1690 — An English fleet attacks French settlements along the St. Lawrence River, raiding and burning Jolliet's estate on Anticosti Island

1691 — Jolliet rebuilds his settlement on Anticosti Island, but the English burn it again

1694 — Jolliet returns to Labrador and maps parts of northeastern Canada

1695 — Jolliet sails to France and presents his own maps to King Louis XIV

1696 — King Louis appoints Jolliet Royal Hydrographer for the Quebec colony; Jolliet begins teaching chartmaking at the Jesuit College in Quebec

1700 — Louis Jolliet dies in the summer in the Quebec region

Glossary of Terms

ailment — A disease

alder — A tree or shrub of the birch family that grows in moist ground

ascend — To rise; to ascend a river is to travel against the current—that is, away from its mouth and toward its source

broth — A liquid in which meat or vegetables have been cooked

buckskin — Leather clothing material made from the skin of a male deer

callused — Having thickened or hardened skin

captive — Someone captured and held as a prisoner

catgut — A strong cord usually made from sheep intestines

cauldron — A large kettle

christen — To baptize and give a name, or simply to name

conquistador — A conqueror, especially the Spanish conquerors in the New World

converse — To talk together; to have a conversation

cottonwood — A tree with abundant foliage

cypress — An evergreen tree of the pine family

disposition — Mood, temper, or state of mind

dysentery — An infectious disease causing severe diarrhea

esteem — To value highly

fatigue — Tiredness, exhaustion

fervor — Intense feeling, devotion, or passion

forge — A furnace or workshop for making things out of iron

harpsichord — An instrument similar to a grand piano but smaller, having two keyboards, and making a softer sound

helmsman — The person who steers a boat by operating a wheel or lever connected to the rudder

inconvenience — Trouble, annoyance

latitude — One's position in terms of north or south, figured according to imaginary east-west lines around the earth parallel to the equator

migratory — Moving from one region to another, usually depending on the climate and the availability of food

musket — A large, heavy gun, usually carried leaning on the shoulder

oilskin — Cloth that has been treated with oil to make it waterproof

parchment — Sheets of sheep or goat skin that can be written upon

pilgrimage — A trip to a religious shrine or holy place

render — To melt something in order to remove a substance from it

renowned — Famous

rosin — A sticky or hardened substance that comes from pine wood

sentinel — Someone who stands watch; a guard or sentry

sloop — A boat with one mast, usually with one sail ahead of the mast and one behind it

stocking cap — A long, knitted, cone-shaped winter cap

sturgeon — A large, long fish with hard scales

surgeon — A doctor who performs surgery

tresses — Locks or braids of hair

tundra — A treeless plain in cold regions, having frozen ground under its dark, moist surface soil

typhoid fever — A disease marked by fever, diarrhea, and severe headaches

universal — Occurring or present everywhere

venison — Deer meat

zeal — Enthusiasm, passion

Bibliography

For Further Reading

Baker, Susan. *Explorers of North America*. Milwaukee: Raintree, 1990.

Carson, Robert. *Hernando De Soto: Expedition to the Mississippi River*. Chicago: Childrens Press, 1991.

Hargrove, Jim. *René-Robert Cavelier, Sieur de La Salle: Explorer of the Mississippi River*. Chicago: Childrens Press, 1990.

Lomask, Milton. *Great Lives: Exploration*. New York: Macmillan, 1988.

Ryan, Peter. *Explorers and Mapmakers*. New York: Dutton, 1990.

Tanner, Helen Horbeck, ed. *Atlas of Great Lakes Indian History*. Norman: University of Oklahoma Press, 1987.

Wolfson, Evelyn. *From Abenaki to Zuni: A Dictionary of Native American Tribes*. New York: Walker & Company, 1988.

Zandra, Dan. *Explorers of America: DeSoto*. Mankato, MN: Creative Education, 1988.

Index

Page numbers in boldface type indicate illustrations.

Picture Acknowledgments

The Bettmann Archive — 2 (left), 4, 5, 76, 118

Brown Brothers — 42, 56

©Cameramann International, Ltd. — 103

Culver Pictures, Inc. — 22

Steven Gaston Dobson — Cover illustration

Illinois State Historical Society — 26-27

National Archives of Canada — 14 (C-002900), 111 (C-006022)

North Wind Picture Archives — 2 (right), 6–7, 12–13, 23, 25, 31, 33, 35, 37, 38-39, 40, 43, 46, 48, 50, 53, 54–55, 58, 61, 62, 69, 82, 86–87, 92, 94, 112–113, 115, 116

R/C Photo Agency:©Richard Capps — 10, 52

Stock Montage — 9, 11, 15, 20, 60, 73, 89, 100, 119

Tony Stone Images: ©Terry Farmer — 66–67

Valan Photos: ©Deborah Vanslit — 8; ©Kennon Cooke — 18–19; ©Wayne Lankinen — 24, 80–81; ©Robert LaSalle — 28-29, 104–105; ©Joseph R. Pearce — 90–91; ©Francis Lepine — 109

©Dr. Harry E. Wood, artist/First Financial Bank, Stevens Point, Wisconsin — 71

Lindaanne Donohoe — Maps on pages 47, 51, 79, 98, 101

About the Author

Zachary Kent grew up in Little Falls, New Jersey, graduated from St. Lawrence University, and holds a teaching certificate in English. He worked for a New York City literary agency for two years before launching his writing career. To support himself while writing, he has worked as a taxi driver, a shipping clerk, and a house painter. Mr. Kent has had a lifelong interest in history. His special hobby as a boy was the study of United States presidents. His collection of presidential items includes books, pictures, and games, as well as several autographed letters.